© **Copyright Smart Cookie Publishing 2023 - All rights reserved.**
The content contained within this book may not be reproduced, duplicated or
transmitted without direct written permission from the author or the publisher.
Under no circumstances will any blame or legal responsibility be held against the publisher, or author, for any damages, reparation, or monetary loss due to the information contained within this book. Either directly or indirectly. You are responsible for your own choices, actions, and results.

Legal Notice:
This book is copyright protected. This book is only for personal use. You cannot amend, distribute, sell, use, quote or paraphrase any part, or the content within this book, without the consent of the author or publisher.

Disclaimer Notice:
Please note the information contained within this document is for educational and entertainment purposes only. All effort has been executed to present accurate, up to date, and reliable, complete information. No warranties of any kind are declared or implied. Readers acknowledge that the author is not engaging in the rendering of legal, financial, medical or professional advice. The content within this book has been derived from various sources. Please consult a licensed professional before attempting any techniques outlined in this book.

By reading this document, the reader agrees that under no circumstances is the author responsible for any losses, direct or indirect, which are incurred as a result of the use of the information contained within this document, including (but not limited to) errors, omissions, or inaccuracies.

Special thanks to Jan, you know who you are!

That's Bonkers!

CONTENTS

INTRODUCTION		PAGE 1
CHAPTER 1	Poop, Slime and All Things Gross	PAGE 3
CHAPTER 2	You Didn't Know Ancient Egypt Was So Weird	PAGE 7
CHAPTER 3	Nope Math Is Not Boring	PAGE 11
CHAPTER 4	Animals That Want To Eat You	PAGE 15
CHAPTER 5	What You Have Never Been Taught In Science	PAGE 19
CHAPTER 6	Amazing Inventions	PAGE 23
CHAPTER 7	Secrets About Bears That Noone Knows	PAGE 27
CHAPTER 8	My Body Does WHAT?	PAGE 31
CHAPTER 9	Other Countries, Religion, Culture & Habits	PAGE 35
CHAPTER 10	The Hidden Life Of Sharks	PAGE 39
CHAPTER 11	Where Are Those Weird Places?	PAGE 43
CHAPTER 12	Kings, Castles And Treasures	PAGE 47
CHAPTER 13	What The Heck Is Up There?	PAGE 51
CHAPTER 14	Stop Bugging Me!	PAGE 55
CHAPTER 15	Rivers, Lakes And Oceans	PAGE 59
CHAPTER 16	Strange But True Animal Facts	PAGE 63
CHAPTER 17	You Won't Believe Your Eyes!	PAGE 69
CHAPTER 18	Could You Have Survived In Prehistoric Times?	PAGE 73
CHAPTER 19	Things Your Parents Don't Even Know (ask them and you'll see!)	PAGE 77
CHAPTER 20	Fantastic Natural Phenomena	PAGE 81
CHAPTER 21	Unexplained Mysteries	PAGE 85
CHAPTER 22	You Had No Clue This Happened	PAGE 89
CHAPTER 23	Food For Thought	PAGE 91
CHAPTER 24	Watch Your Tongue	PAGE 97
CHAPTER 25	Hacks, Tips And Tricks	PAGE 101
CHAPTER 26	Zoom, Zoom, Zoom!	PAGE 105
CHAPTER 27	Guts And Glory	PAGE 109
CHAPTER 28	Artsy Fartsy	PAGE 113
CHAPTER 29	You Are My Hero	PAGE 115
CHAPTER 30	Explosions And Eruptions	PAGE 119
CHAPTER 31	Mashed Potatoes	PAGE 123

That's Bonkers!

INTRODUCTION

Knowing things is fun. Knowing more things is more fun, and the world has an almost endless supply of things to know!

From the gross to the great, this book of facts will surely blow your mind away and is something that will even amaze parents and teachers around you. You will have fun entertaining them with all your new knowledge. So get ready to read and share some of the coolest facts about our world.

Here are just some of the amazing things you are about to discover:

- What important things that can be made using bat poop
- The size of an Ostrich's brain
- What special extra settings do astronauts have on their toilets that we don't
- The number of times lightning strikes our planet
- How many times your heart beats in a day
- The amazing list of animals that want to eat you
- The disgusting origins of some of your favorite food

All this and so much more is waiting for you here. So be prepared to be amazed, entertained, fascinated, and completely surprised

There is stuff here that you didn't know. There is also stuff you might have thought you knew but didn't have quite right. Kings and castles, sharks and bears, stars and planets, giraffes and bacteria, and a few tips to use in your daily life and around the house thrown in for good measure. A wide sampling of everything the universe has to offer, right at your fingertips

Have fun!

That's Bonkers!

That's Bonkers!

Chapter 1

POOP, SLIME AND ALL THINGS GROSS

1. Did you know that bat poop is called guano and can be used to make gunpowder and explosives?

2. Office desks usually have 400 times more bacteria on them than toilet seats.

3. Our noses make more snot when it is cold to try to warm up the air we are breathing.

4. Those cute pandas everyone likes so much are pooping up to 50 times a day.

5. Did you know that human poop is made up of almost 75% water?

6. For over 60 days, in 1858, the city of London smelled like poop because of a sewage problem.

7. Llama poop has almost no odor, and llama farmers call llama poop "llama beans".

8. You will shed around 600,000 particles of skin each hour. That means that by the time you are 70, you will have lost 105 pounds of skin.

9. Did you know that frogs eat their skin after they shed it?

10. Sea sponges squeeze out the mucus to get rid of their waste.

11. The average human will make over 34 ounces (1 liter) of snot per day.

12. The average human also produces around 1 to 2 liters of saliva per day.

That's Bonkers!

POOP SLIME AND ALL THINGS GROSS

13. The average person farts 14 times a day.

14. Dung beetles love to eat poop. They love it so much that they push it around in little balls. It's like a portable snack for them!

15. People have used cow poop to build houses. They have also burned it to cook and heat their homes. Some have even used it as a hockey puck in the winter

16. A person will poop a pile as big as a car in their lifetime.

17. A long time ago, pee was part of the process of making leather. Someone making leather would even purchase other people's pee for this purpose.

18. The main job of snot is to keep dust from getting into our lungs.

19. Animal poop can also be called dung or scat.

20. A lobster's bladder is located underneath its brain, and they sometimes will squirt pee at each other to communicate.

21. Did you know that elephants produce over 300 pounds of poop a day?!

22. Did you know that one very expensive coffee bean comes only from animal poop?

23. You can fill a balloon with the amount of gas you fart in one day.

24. People in the Middle Ages didn't take baths. They thought it was healthier to stay dirty!

25. Doctors used to put leeches on people to try to cure diseases. They still do in some countries.

26. Male hippos flip their tails around to spray their poop all over the place.

4

That's Bonkers!

POOP SLIME AND ALL THINGS GROSS

27. Tiny little mites live on your eyelashes. They are always there.

28. Right now, over 1 million bacteria are in your mouth!

29. One of the dirtiest things in your home is your TV remote control. It has more germs on it than your toilet seat.

30. The corpse flower smells like rotting meat on purpose. That is how it attracts insects that will then spread its pollen.

31. One out of every ten kids admits to chewing their toe-nails.

32. Most of the dust in your house is made of dead skin.
33. Mother Koalas feed poop to their young ones.

34. Did you know that wearing headphones for just an hour will increase the number of bacteria in your ears by 700 times?

35. Vultures poop on their legs to cool off when they get too hot.

36. Do you think spit is gross? You will make enough of that gross stuff to fill 500 bathtubs in your lifetime!

37. When you drink apple or orange juice, there are proba-bly some squished-up maggots in there.

38. Flushing the toilet with the lid up can spray poop and pee out of the toilet.

39. Dead insects, and even rats or mice, sometimes make it into food at factories.

40. A man in India had a six-foot-long tapeworm removed from his intestines.

41. In ancient Rome, they used urine as mouthwash.

That's Bonkers!

POOP SLIME AND ALL THINGS GROSS

42. Many perfumes have animal pee or poop in them.

43. Eye crusties are primarily dead skin and mucus.

44. Did you know that because astronauts get sick often in space they have a special "vomit-setting" on their toilets?

45. Snot from your nose drains directly into your throat and stomach.

46. That nasty taste in your mouth when you wake up is the result of millions of tiny microbes eating food stuck in your teeth.

47. Did you know that bacteria can grow and divide every twenty minutes? At that pace, one bacterial cell could turn into sixteen million.

48. If you wear a ring, the number of germs living under it could be as high as the population of Europe!

49. Believe it or not, there are approximately 150 pieces of bugs and 5 rodent hairs in one pound of peanut butter!

That's Bonkers!

YOU DIDN'T KNOW

ANCIENT EGYPT
WAS SO WEIRD

Chapter 2

50. One thousand years ago, an Egyptian leader tried to decimate the Great Pyramids of Giza. He gave up after about a year, with only a tiny section of the smallest pyramid missing.

51. One Egyptian Pharaoh named Pepi II ruled for 90 years. He became the ruler of Egypt when he was only six years old.

52. No one alive knows how to pronounce the ancient Egyptian language. All we have today are guesses.

53. The eyes of The Great Sphinx are as tall as a full-grown man.

54. Bowling can be traced back to Egyptian times over 5,000 years ago!

55. The real pharaohs looked nothing like their statues. By looking at their mummies, we know they tended to be overweight.

56. Ancient Egyptian writing uses over 700 symbols. We only have to remember 26!

57. The weight of the Great Pyramid of Egypt is estimated to be 6,648,000 tons.

58. It took over 23 years to build The Great Pyramid.

59. Next time you eat a breath mint, you're eating something invented in ancient Egypt.

That's Bonkers!

YOU DIDN'T KNOW ANCIENT EGYPT WAS SO WEIRD

65. Black cats were believed to bring luck in ancient Egypt.

60. The first toothpaste recipe came from ancient Egypt and was made with rock salt, mint, dried Iris flower, and pepper.

71. At one point in history, mummies were stolen and ground up for magic potions and elixirs.

66. It seems the people of ancient Egypt enjoyed playing board games. Several examples have been found in tombs throughout Egypt. We even have rules for some of them.

72. The Egyptians seemed to like cats quite a bit. They even turned some cats into mummies just the same way they did with important people in Egypt.

61. The Pharaohs like to stay shaved - sometimes even their eyebrows! Although, that didn't stop them from wearing fake beards sometimes.

67. Egyptians used a plant called papyrus to make paper, rope, and even sandals for people to wear.

73. When making a mummy, all of the organs needed to be removed. Do you know how they took the brain out? They would pull it out through the nose.

62. The Egyptians invented locks for doors, but some of their keys were up to two feet long. Try to put that on your keychain!

68. Even before they learned how to make wheels, the Egyptians were using boats on the Nile river to move large loads across the kingdom.

63. Ancient Egyptians commonly wore makeup. Both women and men routinely put on makeup and perfumes in daily life.

74. There is evidence that a hippo killed King Tut!

69. Many of the ancient Egyptian gods had animal heads. Their most important god, Ra, had the head of a hawk.

64. Over 60 pharaohs are buried near King Tut in The Valley of the Kings.

75. There were over 2,000 different gods worshiped in ancient Egypt. That's a lot of Gods to remember, don't you think?

70. King Tut was buried with a lock of his grandmother's hair.

8

That's Bonkers!

YOU DIDN'T KNOW ANCIENT EGYPT WAS SO WEIRD

76. Wealthy Egyptians sometimes bathed in sour milk to make their skin softer.

77. There may be hidden rooms in the pyramids we don't yet know about.

78. The Great Sphinx is one of the oldest - and largest - statues left in the world.

79. The Pyramid of Khufu was the tallest building in the world for over 3,700 years.

80. The pyramids of Giza used to have white, smooth sides. It is believed that at least one of them was capped in gold.

81. There are over 130 different pyramids in Egypt

82. Cleopatra was the queen of Egypt but wasn't an Egyptian herself. She was Greek.

83. There are over 2.3 million blocks in the great pyramid.

84. The ancient Egyptians divided the year into three seasons. They had summer, winter, and flood seasons when the Nile river crossed its banks.

85. Egyptian brewers invented the straw to taste their beer without disturbing the fermenting ingredients that floated on top of the container.

86. King Tut was only nine years old when he became Pharaoh.

87. Egyptians drank beer daily. It was a huge part of their diet.

88. Egyptians were the first to use paper for much of their writing.

89. Pharaohs kept their hair covered so that it was hidden from regular Egyptians.

90. Mummies would be covered in as much as a mile of wrapping.

91. The world's largest pyramid is in Cholula de Rivadavia near Mexico City, not Egypt!

That's Bonkers!

That's Bonkers!

NOPE, MATH is NOT BORING

Chapter 3

92. Any whole number multiplied by an even number will give you another even number as the answer. The only way to get an odd number from multiplication is to multiply two odd numbers.

93. The company Google is named after a number. A "googol" is a number 1 followed by 100 zeros

94. Mathematicians say there is more than one type of infinity, and some infinities are bigger than others.

95. Humans have been doing math for over 32,000 years.

96. The Roman numeral system has no way to represent zero.

97. There are 86,400 seconds in every day.

98. It is almost guaranteed that two people will share the same birthday in any group of 50 people.

99. You cannot divide a number by zero. Ever.

100. If you add 2 to any even number, the answer will always be even. Add two to an odd number, and the answer will always be odd.

That's Bonkers! + − × ÷ = ≠ ≈ π

NOPE MATH IS NOT BORING

101. There is a word for people that are afraid of numbers. They have Arithmophobia.

106. 2 and 5 are the only prime numbers that end in a two or a five.

111. A penny doubled every day for one month would come to $5,368,709.12!!!

102. Did you know that a dime has 118 ridges around the edge?

107. Also, there are no prime numbers that end with a zero.

112. If you add up the numbers from 1 to 100, you get 5050.

103. People in East Asia think 4 is an unlucky number.

108. Most of the geometry books used in school are based on an ancient Greek textbook by a man named Euclid.

113. Math was used to break German codes during World War II.

104. 4 is the only number that has the same amount of letters as its value.

109. Math likely got started so people could tell time and following seasons.

114. You can only evenly divide prime numbers by one and themselves.

105. The word "hundred" comes from an old Norse word that meant 120 instead of 100. Talk about inaccurate descriptions!

110. Everything a computer does is done with mathematics.

115. Some mathematicians study almost nothing but prime numbers.

± ∞ Ø Σ < > √ % ± ∞ *That's Bonkers!*

NOPE! MATH IS NOT BORING

116. There is an 'e' in every odd number, like one, three, five, seven, and nine.

117. Imaginary, complex, and irrational are examples of different types of numbers.

118. If you add up the digits of 9 times any other number, they will equal 9. For example, 9 X 5 = 45. 4 + 5 = 9. Try it!

119. A group in ancient Greece thought numbers explained the gods.

120. Einstein claimed he was not very good at math.

121. Isaac Newton invented calculus.

122. Without geometry and mathematics, there would be no video games.

123. The number zero was first used in India.

124. Alex Eskin won a $3 million prize - for doing mathematics.

125. A number that reads the same backward and forward is called a Palindrome number. An example of this is 12821.

126. There are precisely 43,252,003,274,489,856,000 ways to scramble a Rubik's Cube.

That's Bonkers + − × ÷ = ≠ ≈ π < >   13

That's Bonkers!

Chapter 4

ANIMALS THAT WANT TO EAT YOU

127. In the 1980s, India's tigers killed as many as 60 people a year. Most of these people were going into the woods to gather firewood. When the woodcutters began wearing masks on the back of their heads, the tigers thought they were watching them and stopped attacking.

128. Hippos are responsible for twice as many human deaths each year as lions. But hippos don't eat us. Lions will.

129. Of all the animals in the world, only about 15 are known to attack people for anything other than self-defense.

130. Crocodiles seem to think of you as a tasty meal, while other animals prefer food other than people.

131. Did you know that tigers can run at over 30 miles per hour?

132. Almost all recorded shark attacks involve only a single bite. It seems they don't like the way we taste.

133. Every year, dogs kill more people in the U.S. than great white sharks have in the past hundred years!

134. An octopus has no interest in eating you, but if its life is uninteresting or it is kept in a small place, it will sometimes eat its legs out of boredom.

135. Both rats and pigs have been known to eat defenceless people.

That's Bonkers!

ANIMALS THAT WANT TO EAT YOU

136. There have been only a few documented cases of piranhas attacking or eating people. It seems the little fish somehow got a bad reputation.

137. A vampire bat will drink up to half of its body weight in blood every night. Yum!

138. Dermestid beetles in North America feed on the dead bodies of people and other animals.

139. In the 1700s, a wolf in France called the Beast of Gévaudan is said to have killed over 100 people.

140. Hyenas are mostly scavengers, but that doesn't mean they won't scavenge injured humans.

141. Mosquitoes use the carbon dioxide we breathe out to find us.

142. The movie Jaws was inspired by an actual shark that is said to have killed four people and injured 7. The attacks were in 1917 along the coast of New York State.

143. A grizzly bear ate a man and his girlfriend in Alaska after they lived with the bears for 13 summers.

144. Killer whales have never killed a human that we know of in the wild. They don't want to eat us!

145. Did you know that Tigers have killed more people than any other large cat?

146. Lice are another human blood drinker that many kids have contact with in school.

147. Did you know that a wolf can eat up to 20 pounds of meat in just one meal? That's a whole lot of meat!

148. Pet dogs and a few cats have eaten their owners' bodies after they had died.

149. Giant catfish in the Amazon river are suspected of eating people.

That's Bonkers!

ANIMALS THAT WANT TO EAT YOU

150. Lions, Tigers, and Leopards are three cats known to eat people.

151. A lion does not have much time to eat a person because it sleeps for 20 hours a day!

152. Dingos have only attacked people twice that we know of, and they were small children.

153. We don't know why, but spotted hyenas are more likely to attack people than striped hyenas.

154. We talked about crocodiles eating people, but alligators usually choose to stay away from humans.

155. The reticulated python is the longest snake in the world, the largest being 33 feet long. They can eat bears, deer, wild hogs, and probably a human.

156. Guess what was found in the stomach of a python in 2017? That's right, a human!

157. Lions are more likely to attack at night after a full moon.

158. Rodents have been known to eat their way into a dead human body.

159. Not only will Komodo Dragons attack people, but they will also dig up graves to eat dead people.

160. A Polish pig farmer was completely eaten by his pigs after dying on his farm. Only the bones were left.

161. There are dust mites constantly feeding on your dead skin.

162. Botflies' larvae burrow into human skin. The skin is their food until they become adult flies.

163. Coyotes have been seen attacking children, but this is extremely rare.

That's Bonkers!

ANIMALS THAT WANT TO EAT YOU

164. Ticks bury their heads into people and animals to get to their blood.

165. Leeches can drink almost ten times their body weight of your blood in one feeding.

166. One bear in India killed at least 12 people in 1957.

That's Bonkers!

WHAT YOU HAVE NEVER BEEN TAUGHT IN SCIENCE

Chapter 5

167. Scientists still don't agree on what it means to say something is "alive."

168. No one can truly explain why we yawn.

169. The wind is silent and makes no sound at all. It only makes a sound when it blows against an obstacle or an object.

170. Did you know it is possible for water to both freeze and boil at the same time?

171. An average weight adult would weigh around 250 tons on the sun!

172. Sound moves around four times faster while traveling in water than through the air.

173. Christopher Columbus probably already knew the Earth was round. It wasn't something he "discovered."

174. Many dinosaurs had feathers.

175. A sunset on Mars appears blue instead of red.

176. Astronomers use a planet's gravity to determine how much the planet weighs.

That's Bonkers!   HUBBLE BUBBLE BOIL AND TROUBLE

WHAT YOU HAVE NEVER BEEN TAUGHT IN SCIENCE

177. The United States has more tornadoes yearly than any other country on the planet.

178. The bacteria cells in our bodies outnumber human cells.

179. Almost 75% of the food we eat comes from 10-15 plant species and only five animal species.

180. Clouds look light and fluffy floating in the air. But the water in them is heavy. Very very heavy.

181. Did you know that every year, the moon moves 1 inch away from the Earth? Because of this, someday, we won't have solar eclipses anymore.

182. Humans are the only animals with a chin.

183. If every star in the Milky Way were a grain of salt, they would fill an Olympic-sized swimming pool.

184. We have discovered 63 moons orbiting Jupiter, and there may still be more undiscovered.

185. Sound waves create heat in the air that they pass through.

186. Teeth are the only body part that can not heal.

187. Things that sink below the surface of the water can end up floating deeper down and never reach the bottom.

188. Mercury is liquid at room temperature.

20   HUBBLE BUBBLE BOIL AND TROUBLE   *That's Bonkers!*

WHAT YOU HAVE NEVER BEEN TAUGHT IN SCIENCE

189. You will still sweat when underwater if you get too hot.

190. Scientists have figured out a way to turn leftover plastic into vanilla flavoring using bacteria.

191. Some people are choosing to have their dead bodies, or just their brains, frozen in the hope that they can be revived in the future.

192. George Washington had dentures – but they were definitely not made of wood.

193. Human bodies glow. We give off our own light, but it is too dim for us to see with our naked eyes.

194. More men are colorblind than women.

195. The melting of the polar ice caps has a measurable impact on Earth's gravity.

196. Weirdly enough, hot water freezes faster than cold water!

197. Your weight changes under different gravity, but your mass stays the same.

198. Bees flap their wings over 200 times a second.

199. Drinking too much water can kill you.

200. The magnetic poles of the Earth seem to reverse randomly. The last time was almost 800,000 years ago. The next time could be tomorrow.

That's Bonkers!   HUBBLE BUBBLE BOIL AND TROUBLE

WHAT YOU HAVE NEVER BEEN TAUGHT IN SCIENCE

201. You'll have lost about half of your taste buds by the time you are 60 years old.

202. This sounds weird, but working in a nuclear power plant is safer than in a typical office.

203. Scientists think that gas planets like Jupiter or Saturn may have rain showers of diamonds in their atmospheres.

204. Tomatoes have more genes in their DNA than humans do.

205. In Germany, they have potty-trained cows so they can control where their pee goes and protect the environment.

206. The hardest metal known is tungsten, and it is almost impossible to melt.

207. The only letter that does not appear in the periodic table is the letter J.

208. A person will walk the equivalent of five times around the equator in their lifetime.

209. Plants watered with warm water grow larger and quicker than those watered with cold water.

210. A lead pencil can draw a 35 miles (56 km) long line.

211. If you put two straws in your mouth, with one inside a drink and the other outside of it, you won't be able to drink through either straw.

HUBBLE BUBBLE BOIL AND TROUBLE   That's Bonkers!

Chapter 7

AMAZING INVENTIONS

212. Thomas Edison patented the lightbulb, but Humphrey Davy actually made the first electric light.

213. Thomas Edison did give us the record player and movie projector.

214. The first bicycles didn't have a chain or brakes. Scary huh?!

215. A 10-year-old named Richie Stachowski invented a mask that lets swimmers talk to each other underwater.

216. Did you know that a 16-year-old invented the trampoline in 1930? Cool or what?

217. Benjamin Franklin invented bifocal eyeglasses.

218. Another famous child inventor was Louis Braille. He invented the system of raised dots as writing for people who are blind, which is now named after him.

219. Did you know that windmills were invented around 2,000 BC? China and Persia were the first to build and use them.

220. It seems hard to believe, but the wheel had to be invented by someone. Our world would not exist without it.

221. The printing press was an invention that allowed people to write about other inventions. Because of that, it may be one of the most important inventions since writing.

That's Bonkers!

AMAZING INVENTIONS

222. Speaking of writing, that seems to have been invented in ancient Sumeria to keep track of farm goods being traded.

223. Modern writing changed with the invention of the ballpoint pen by John J. Loud in 1888.

224. Teenager Dasia Taylor invented a suture that tells if wounds are infected. The suture will change color to indicate if your wound is infected.

225. Alexander Graham Bell is said to have invented the telephone, however, it seems that others had the same idea.

226. Batteries were first demonstrated by a man named Volta, which is why we measure electricity in Volts today.

227. The internet was originally invented as a way for the United States Military to communicate during wartime.

228. Believe it or not, zippers didn't exist until just before 1900.

229. Did you know that the first headphones were created in 1910?

230. The bulletproof vest was invented by a pizza delivery guy who had been shot twice. I guess he was afraid to be shot a third time!

231. Believe it or not, the inventor of the TV was named Philo Farnsworth and that he developed the concept when he was only fourteen years old.

232. The nails used to fasten wood were invented over 5,500 years ago.

233. The Chinese made the first compasses.

234. Let's not forget that someone had to invent gunpowder. That seems to have been in the 900s - somewhere in China.

24

That's Bonkers!

AMAZING INVENTIONS

235. The inventor of the lawnmower wasn't sure if people would laugh at his invention, so he always tested it at night when nobody could see it.

236. One of the first computers was the size of a tennis court.

237. It took over 20 years of work to get bubble gum right.

238. Scottish inventor James Watt finally put the finishing touches on a working steam engine. This led the way to modern gasoline engines.

239. Karl Benz is credited with inventing the automobile in 1885. Yup, he is the Benz from today's Mercedes Benz brand of cars.

240. Automobiles existed before gas-powered tractors were used on farms.

241. The Super Soaker squirt gun was invented in 1990.

242. The first working calculator didn't have any batteries. It was mechanical, not electronic.

243. The first balloons were made of animal intestines.

244. The first microwaves were not called microwaves. Instead, they were called Radar Ranges.

245. The guy who invented velcro got the idea from the burrs stuck in his dog's fur after a hunting trip.

246. Did you know that lighters were actually invented before matches?

247. It took several decades after people started putting food in tin cans before someone invented the modern-style can opener. I wonder what they used to open their cans before that invention?

That's Bonkers! 25

That's Bonkers!

SECRETS ABOUT BEARS THAT NOONE KNOWS

Chapter 7

248. Some bears in North America hibernate for eight months out of the year. They don't leave their den at all during that time.

249. Not all Polar bears hibernate, just pregnant females. Their den is called a "Maternity Den." The hibernation of these pregnant females is not as deep as other bears, as they only lower their temperature to conserve energy to make milk for their cubs.

250. Bears can catch fish with their paws.

251. Did you know that a male Polar bear can weigh as much as ten adult men?

252. Baby bears are called cubs.

253. Bears will break into cars and cabins in search of food.

254. Black bears are not always black. They can be white, gray, or brown.

255. Bears are born blind, just like puppies and kittens.

That's Bonkers!

SECRETS ABOUT BEARS THAT NOONE KNOWS

256. Almost all bears can stand on their hind legs.

261. The oldest known polar bear lived for 42 years. The oldest known black bear died after 39 years.

265. Grizzly bears are only about the size of a chipmunk at birth.

257. No other animal hunts bear except people.

262. Scientists used to think pandas were not actual bears, but we now know that they are.

266. King Henry the 3rd was given a polar bear. He kept his pet bear on a long chain so that he could roam around the palace. His bear could even go into the backyard and catch fish from a little creek.

258. The Polar bear's fur is not white but transparent, and the strands of hair of the outer coat are hollow.

263. Polar bears do not drink water. They primarily eat fat, which releases water when it is digested. It is through this process that Polar bears stay hydrated.

259. Polar bears are excellent swimmers. They can swim at speeds of up to 6mph and approximately 62 miles without taking a break!

264. A polar bear can hold its breath for up to 3 minutes.

267. Asiatic black bears can walk for miles on two legs.

260. Most bears are omnivorous except Polar bears, which are primarily carnivorous. Their diet consists mainly of seals and sometimes berries, kelp, and vegetation, when necessary.

268. Can you believe that Polar bears have black skin? This helps them absorb the sun's heat.

That's Bonkers!

SECRETS ABOUT BEARS THAT NOONE KNOWS

269. Most bears have 42 teeth, and we only have 32.

274. Currently, there are only eight different species of bears alive.

277. Brown bears have been seen using stone tools.

270. The Kodiak bear is the largest species of bear, and the Sun bear is the smallest.

275. Unique dumpsters and garbage cans have been designed for places where bears and people are neighbors. It can get very messy when a bear can open a garbage can!

278. Polar bears are generally a solitary species, but some adult male Polar bears can form friendships that last for months! They will play-fight together, feed together, and travel together.

271. Once, a bear named Wojtek, was enlisted in the Polish army and made it to the rank of Corporal. He carried water, alcohol, and weapons to the front lines during battles.

272. Polar bears don't seem to be afraid of anything - including people and sometimes even gunshots.

276. A black bear has a better sense of smell than a dog.

P279. Did you know that only female Polar bears can be tracked using radio collars? The males' necks are larger than their heads, so the tracking devices fall off!

273. Grizzly and Polar bear cubs spend two years with their mom before venturing out on their own.

280. Black bears have between 1 and 5 pups per litter. Three is the most common.

SECRETS ABOUT BEARS THAT NOONE KNOWS

281. Koala bears are not bears at all. They are marsupials. Did you know that they have a pouch like a Kangaroo?

282. Did you know that a group of pandas is called an "embarrassment"?

283. Baloo, from the movie The Jungle Book, is a Sloth bear. Sloth bears are found in India, Sri Lanka, and Nepal. They are pretty cute - you should check them out.

284. Sloth bears are the only bears carrying their cubs on their backs, maybe because they spend a lot of time eating fruit in the trees. Their other favorite foods are ants and termites.

285. The Atlas bear of north Africa went extinct in the late 1800s. It was mainly herbivorous, approximately 9 feet long, and could weigh up to 1000 pounds.

286. Bear fur comprises two coats: A short coat for warmth and a long coat to keep out water and ice. The Polar bear has the thickest and most warm coats of all bears.

287. Doctors and scientists are trying to see if they can make people hibernate like bears. This could help treat injuries and make space travel more comfortable for people.

288. Adult male bears are called boars.

That's Bonkers!

MY BODY DOES WHAT?!?

Chapter 8

294. Are you aware that your heart is about the size of your fist?

289. Your heart beats about 100,000 times every single day.

295. Did you know that a person blinks approximately 20 times per minute? Amazingly, we don't even notice.

290. You will probably drink enough water in your life to fill a good-sized swimming pool.

296. You'll never touch your elbow with your tongue or nose. Try it!

291. If laid out, end to end, veins, and arteries in an adult body could circle the Earth twice.

297. You use over 40 muscles to smile and 200 different muscles for walking.

292. You are born with 300 bones. Adults have only 206 because some of those bones naturally grow together throughout your life.

298. Did you realize that it's impossible to breathe and swallow at the same time?

293. What is the strongest muscle in your body? The Masseter, it is responsible for lifting your jaw.

That's Bonkers!

MY BODY DOES WHAT?!?

299. If you could capture all the electricity in your brain, you could power a light bulb.

300. The average person will sleep for 20-30 years of their life.

301. A human nose can detect over a TRILLION different scents!

302. The small intestine is the largest organ inside your body, but your integumentary system (skin, nails, and hair) is the largest organ of all.

303. Did you know that your feet have one-quarter of all the bones in your body?

304. You have over 600 muscles in your body.

305. The rumbling and gurgling noises made by your stomach are called borborygmus. The noises are created by liquid and gas moving in your stomach and intestines.

306. Once you hit puberty, your bones stop growing in length.

307. You have no muscles in your fingers. All the muscles that control your fingers are in your forearm and palm.

308. You automatically close your eyes every time you sneeze.

309. Your brain will use 20% of the oxygen you breathe.

310. The average person will flex their finger's joints 24 million times in their lifetime.

311. How strong are your bones? As strong as steel.

312. When you wake up, it may feel like you had a dream all night, when in reality, dreams only last 2 to 3 seconds!

That's Bonkers!

MY BODY DOES WHAT?!?

320. Your body is about 70% water, so you can't survive more than a few days without it.

313. The pattern on our tongue is as unique as our fingerprints.

321. You lose as many as 100 hairs every single day. But don't worry; they will grow back.

314. Sometimes your brain is more active when you are asleep than when you are awake.

322. One woman let her fingernails grow to over 28 feet.

315. After age 30 or so, people start getting shorter instead of taller.

323. Earwax comes from sweat glands.

316. Your eyes do not grow at all after you are born. Your nose and ears never stop, though.

324. Both of your lungs are the same size, right? Nope! Your right lung is larger than your left.

317. The average temperature of your body will slowly get cooler as you get older.

325. One out of every 12,000 babies is born with their heart on the right side instead of the left.

318. The saltiness of the ocean matches almost precisely with the saltiness of your blood.

326. Did you realize that your fingernails grow almost four times faster than your toenails?

319. You can survive up to two months without food. Sleep and water are much more important to you than a tasty snack.

That's Bonkers!

MY BODY DOES WHAT?!?

327. The distance between your fingertips when your arms are spread out equals your height.

328. Men usually have a longer ring finger than an index finger. Women are generally about equal.

329. Sneezes out of your mouth travel at over 100 mph (161 km/h).

330. The tongue is the only muscle in the human body that is attached at only one end.

331. Being tickled might make you laugh but what you are actually experiencing is a form of panic.

332. You had blue eyes when you were born. All babies do.

333. 25 million new cells are produced by your body every second. That is more cells than the population of the U.S. in 15 seconds!

334. As far as we know, no other animals besides us blush.

335. Every drop of blood in your body passes through your heart at least once a minute.

336. You don't feel any pain from damage to your brain.

337. Your stomach can dissolve metal. That's how strong stomach acids are.

338. Humans produce one to two liters of saliva each day!

339. Did you know that a change in temperature in your throat can cause hiccups?

340. When you bump your funny bone, it really hurts! Why would anyone call that a funny bone? It is a play on words, the bone is called the Humerus bone, and it sounds like the word humorous, which means funny

That's Bonkers!

OTHER COUNTRIES, RELIGION, CULTURE & HABITS
Chapter 9

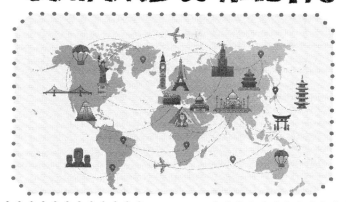

341. In Norway, people use knives and forks to eat pizza, sandwiches and even hamburgers!

342. A town in England has a tradition of chasing cheese rolled down a steep hill. It is a way to celebrate spring.

343. Did you know that New Zealand is the only country in the world with every single type of climate?

344. In Egypt, it is considered bad luck to step on cut hair that has fallen on the floor. What do barbers do?

345. In some cultures, paying for dinner at a restaurant without leaving a tip is rude. In other countries, it is the opposite.

346. There are currently over 4,000 different religions in the world.

347. One group of people on an Atlantic island have used potatoes for money.

348. There are 195 countries in the world.

349. Half of the world follows the three most popular religions; Christianity, Islam, and Hinduism.

350. What is the oldest country in the world? Japan, it has existed for over 2,500 years.

That's Bonkers!

OTHER COUNTRIES, RELIGION, CULTURE & HABITS

351. Did you know that the Sahara desert used to be a tropical rainforest?

352. Forty-four countries have no ocean shores because other countries surround them.

353. Most people think Egypt has the most pyramids, but Sudan has more than twice the amount!

354. The night before a wedding in Germany, friends and family smash dishes in front of the couple's house. The couple then has to clean it up - what a bummer!

355. Men jump over newborn babies in one city in Spain.

356. It is typical for the President of the United States to issue an official pardon to the live turkey delivered to the capital for Thanksgiving dinner. The pardoned turkey is then allowed to live.

357. Four days of the week are named after gods many Vikings would have worshipped. Tuesday, Wednesday, Thursday, and Friday are all inspired by Norse god names.

358. More people live in China than in any other country in the world.

359. One of the animals worshipped by the ancient Mayans was the turkey. It was seen as a vehicle of the gods.

360. The largest forests in the world are in Russia.

361. In some parts of China, the husband carries the new wife over burning coals.

362. People in Cambodia sometimes eat fried tarantulas.

36

That's Bonkers!

OTHER COUNTRIES, RELIGION, CULTURE & HABITS

363. The longest car tunnel in the world is in Norway, which is 15.2 miles long.

364. Viking men used to dye their hair blonde.

365. 5 countries in the world do not have an airport.

366. Viking women were as fierce on the battlefield as men and fought right alongside them.

367. Did you know that the tip of Russia is only 2 miles away from Alaska?

368. The people of Lopburi, Thailand, hold a feast for the monkeys that live in the city.

369. In Austria, there is a sport called Fingerhakeln - finger-pulling.

370. A lot of people were afraid of redheads in ancient Greece. Some believed they turned into vampires after they died!

371. In Turkey, bread is sacred; they believe throwing it out will bring bad luck.

372. People in Denmark get covered in cinnamon on their 25th birthday if they haven't married yet.

373. It is considered rude to write someone's name in red ink in South Korea.

374. New Zealand has five sheep for every person living there.

That's Bonkers!

OTHER COUNTRIES, RELIGION, CULTURE & HABITS

375. Because guinea pigs are prone to loneliness, it's illegal in Switzerland to own just one.

376. Reggae music started in Jamaica.

377. Panama hats are actually made in Ecuador.

378. The Kingdom of Lesotho is a country in Africa, but its neighbor country of South Africa completely surrounds it

379. The average Japanese produces 2.5 pounds of trash per day, while the average American produces a whopping 7.1 pounds per day!

That's Bonkers!

THE HIDDEN LIFE OF SHARKS

Chapter 10

380. Sharks have no bones.

381. Sharks grow new teeth their entire lives.

382. Sharks pee through their skin.

383. There are over 550 types of sharks alive today.

384. The "Big 3" are responsible for most (unprovoked) attacks on humans: The Great White, Tiger, and Bull sharks.

385. A case of shark's eggs is called a mermaid's purse.

386. Sharks spend most of their lives alone.

387. Based on fossils, the shark is believed to have existed for over 400 million years. That would mean they were here 200 million years before dinosaurs!

388. One shark was found that had 50 rows of teeth.

That's Bonkers!

THE HIDDEN LIFE OF SHARKS

389. Manta rays are closely related to sharks, even though they look so different.

390. Did you know that sharks were on Earth before trees?!

391. It's rare, but there is a shark that can walk on land - the Epaulette shark.

392. More people are killed each year by vending machines falling on them than by sharks.

393. It's very sad to think that 75 species of sharks are in danger of extinction.

394. It's true - some sharks can only breathe while they are moving.

395. Megalodon is a prehistoric shark that was almost as long as two city buses.

396. Sharks can take care of themselves from the moment they are born.

397. Sharks can swim down to 10,000 feet deep.

398. Most sharks only eat once every few days.

399. Which sharks are the most dangerous predator in the ocean? The Great White.

400. Sharks rely primarily on their sense of smell when hunting for food.

401. Most shark bites are out of curiosity or "mistaken identity"; however, people don't always live through a "test bite" from a Great White.

402. Some species of sharks glow in the dark.

40

That's Bonkers!

THE HIDDEN LIFE OF SHARKS

403. Sharks have eyelids but don't blink. Instead, they use their eyelids only to protect the eyes when attacking something.

404. Baby sharks are called pups. Probably because adult sharks used to be called "sea dogs."

405. Most sharks live between 20 and 30 years.

406. Some sharks have long noses lined with teeth that look like a saw.

407. Hammerhead sharks can see all the way around themselves at one time.

408. The Hammerhead's main predator is the Killer Whale.

409. Did you know that the Great White shark has the strongest bite of any predator on the planet?

410. Whale shark skin can be 6 inches thick.

411. A shark's skin is rough, like sandpaper.

412. Sharks are unable to make sounds.

413. Great whites will sometimes eat other sharks. They also catch birds that are floating on the surface of the water.

414. The Dwarf Lantern shark is about the size of a human hand.

415. The only sharks that put their heads out of the water are Great Whites.

416. Did you know that dolphins will team up and chase away attacking sharks?

417. A drum, a video camera, a cannonball, and even an entire suit of knight's armor have all been found in shark stomachs!

That's Bonkers!

THE HIDDEN LIFE OF SHARKS

418. One thing that makes bull sharks one of the most dangerous is that they can live in sea-water or fresh water.

419. A great white shark can have over 300 teeth in its mouth.

420. What is the biggest fish in the ocean? The Whale shark, it can grow up to 46-72 feet in length - that is the length of 3 pick-up trucks.

421. Sharks can detect electricity in the water.

That's Bonkers!

Chapter 11

WHERE ARE THOSE WEIRD PLACES?

422. The Great Wall of China can be seen from outer space.

425. There is only one city in the world located on two continents. Istanbul is in both Europe and Asia.

428. Stonehenge is located in England, about 2 hours' drive from London. One of the many amazing things about it is that it took 1000 years to build.

423. Many North Americans escape the cold in the winter to enjoy the sunniest place on Earth - Yuma, Arizona, United States.

426. Spotted Lake Khiluk in British Columbia, Canada, is 365 separate pools.

429. The biggest pyramid in the world isn't in Egypt. It is the Great Pyramid of Cholula in Mexico.

424. The river Caño Cristales in Columbia, known as the "River of Five Colours," is a rainbow of color every summer. You should look online to find out why; it's pretty cool.

427. Even though Vatican City has the word "city" in its name, it is actually a country. With a population of just 518 people, it is the smallest country in the world.

430. A village in the Netherlands has only footpaths and almost four miles of canal. Instead of driving to a friend's house, you could kayak there!

That's Bonkers!

WHERE ARE THOSE WEIRD PLACES?

435. A small town created the Greater Green River Intergalactic Spaceport in Wyoming as an "emergency UFO landing area."

439. The Waitomo Caves of New Zealand are home to glow worms. The worms live on the ceiling and walls, making them look like stars in the night sky inside the dark cave.

431. Wisconsin Dells is a city in Wisconsin known as the Waterpark Capital of the World.

436. Lake Retba in the African nation of Senegal is pink like cotton candy.

432. Tucson, Arizona, has an airplane-wrecking yard in the middle of the desert. Over 4000 full-size military airplanes are parked there.

437. Ringing Rocks Park in Pennsylvania has rocks that sound like a bell when you hit them with a hammer.

440. Home to the Hobbits in Lord of the Rings, Hobbiton is a real place. When they built it for the movie, they made it permanent so people could visit it for years to come.

433. There are over 200 miles of tunnels under Paris, France, called The Catacombs. They are filled with the bones of former residents.

438. The Le Brea Tar Pits are ponds of bubbling crude oil right in the middle of Los Angeles, California.

441. The town of Barrow in Alaska doesn't see a sunrise for 67 days each winter. They also have continual daylight for the same amount of time in the summer.

434. The Darvaza gas crater in Turkmenistan is a crater caused by an underground deposit of natural gas that was set on fire. It has been burning for over 50 years.

44

That's Bonkers!

WHERE ARE THOSE WEIRD PLACES?

442. Did you know that Tasmania has the cleanest and purest air in the world?

445. A 30-foot sculpture of an eyeball is in Dallas, Texas, United States.

447. A mountain peak in Peru is colored in stripes of blue, pink, red, green, and yellow. Scientists are not sure what caused it.

443. A nuclear power plant explosion in the Soviet Union, called the Chernobyl disaster, led to the permanent evacuation of an entire city.

448. There is a legend that the prior owner of the Winchester Mystery House in California thought she had to continually build onto the house to keep ghosts happy. Some doors go nowhere, some stairs end at the ceiling, and many interesting rooms exist.

444. Cat Island, in Japan, is home to only 100 humans. But there are at least ten cats for every person! That's over one thousand cats living on the island.

446. The water in Lake Natron in Africa quickly turns animals that die in it into weird statues.

449. An island in Siberia is covered in hundreds of whale bones. Scientists think that local tribes put them there hundreds of years ago.

That's Bonkers!

46   That's Bonkers!

KINGS, CASTLES AND TREASURES

Chapter 12

454. There have been 62 different kings or queens of England.

450. Windsor Castle in England has been home to English royalty for over 900 years.

455. Malbork Castle Poland is the largest castle in the world.

451. King Charles III of England is the newest King. He became King of England after the death of his mother, Queen Elizabeth II.

456. It is possible that castles were first built to defend against Viking raids.

452. A real person inspired the vampire in the book Dracula. Prince Vlad, or Vlad the Impaler, was a ruler of the people that now live in Romania.

457. Château is the French word for castle.

453. Queen Elizabeth II had been queen for 70 years and 214 days when she died. That makes her the longest-ruling monarch in English history.

458. The Crown Jewels of Ireland were stolen from Dublin Castle in 1907. They haven't been seen since then.

That's Bonkers!

KINGS, CASTLES AND TREASURES

459. There are more than 10,000 castle sites in Europe. Some are in ruins, but many are still occupied.

460. Not a single pirate treasure map has ever been found in real life.

461. There are currently 43 countries in the world that a King or Queen rules.

462. Brissac Chateau is the tallest castle in France.

463. English kings weren't numbered until the rule of William the Conqueror. While there have been 11 kings with the name Edward, 3 of them came before numbering.

464. Some believe the treasure of the Knights Templar was smuggled out of Europe to North America.

465. King Tut's treasure is one of the greatest of any ruler of Egypt. But only because all the others were stolen long ago.

466. England has had eight kings named Henry

467. Predjama Castle in Slovenia is built into a cave on a 400-foot-high cliff.

468. Two different crowns are used during the crowning of an English king or queen.

469. Houska Castle in the Czech Republic is built over a deep hole that some believe to be a gateway to hell. Nazis did experiments on the occult while occupying it during World War II.

470. Most of the Crown Jewels of England were made in 1661.

The Tower of London

48

That's Bonkers!

Kings, Castles and Treasures

478. The zig-zag shapes along the top of castles are called battlements.

471. What is the most haunted castle in Ireland? Leap Castle.

479. Attackers would sometimes try to dig tunnels under the walls of castles.

472. Our image of a castle is usually of a medieval castle. Later renaissance castles looked more like massive houses.

480. Most castles took about ten years to build.

473. One of the newest castles on Earth is Le Château Frontenac in Québec City, Qc, Canada.

481. The four kings in a deck of cards are all based on real-life kings.

474. Château de Chambord is the largest castle in France.

482. Early kings were usually the first to go into battle during a war. Leading the attack from the front was considered a sign of bravery.

475. Armies would sometimes spend years laying siege to a single castle.

483. King Louis XIV had the longest rule of any king or queen in Europe. He ruled for 72 years, starting at age 4.

476. The Tower of London was the first stone tower in London; its construction started in 1070.

484. There is very little evidence that pirates ever actually buried treasure.

477. Many castles have a "murder hole" in the ceiling above the entrance where defenders could drop boiling liquids on attackers.

That's Bonkers!

That's Bonkers!

WHAT THE HECK IS UP THERE?
Chapter 13

485. Astronomers estimate that there are 10,000 stars in the universe for every single grain of sand on planet Earth.

486. Were you aware that the rings of Saturn are mostly ice?

487. It takes nine minutes for the light from the Sun to travel to the Earth and over four years for the light of our closest neighbor star to reach us.

488. You'll weigh six times less on the Moon than you do on Earth

489. Of all eight planets, only one is named after a Greek god: Uranus. All the rest are named after Roman gods.

490. Would you spend 12 million dollars on a suit? NASA did! In 1974 the cost of each space suit was 12 million dollars.

491. Did you know that applesauce was the first food eaten in space?

492. July 4th, 1982, is the first time an astronaut spent the 4th of July in space!

493. Did you know that you could easily fit all of the planets from our solar system between the Earth and the Moon and still have lots of room to spare?

494. Believe it or not, sunsets on Mars are blue!

That's Bonkers!

WHAT THE HECK IS UP THERE?

495. The Sun is big enough to hold over one million Earths.

496. There are around 4,700 satellites in space as of 2023, but only 1,800 are still working.

497. Some astronomers believe there is at least one more planet in our solar system. Until we find it, scientists call the possible planet either Planet X or Planet Nine.

498. We currently know of over 200 moons orbiting the eight planets of our solar system.

499. Jupiter's big red spot is a storm that has been going on for at least 200 years.

500. The Milky Way is what we call our galaxy, but not all people refer to it by that name. "Silver River" is what it is called in China, and "Backbone of Night" is how it is referred to in the Kalahari Desert in Southern Africa.

501. The Moon always looks the same because the same side is always facing us.

502. Many scientists today believe that the Moon was created when Earth collided with another object about the size of Mars. They call this other object Thela.

503. Did you know that Venus spins backward?

504. The atmosphere of Pluto is thicker than the atmosphere of Earth.

505. Uranus is tipped over on its side compared to the rest of the planets.

The International Space Station

52

That's Bonkers!

WHAT THE HECK IS UP THERE?

506. Over 99% of all the matter in our solar system is in the Sun.

507. Some stars spin more than 500 times every second.

508. Shadows are darker and sharper on the Moon.

509. Did you know that even though Venus is not the closest planet to the Sun, it is still the hottest planet in the solar system?

510. Mars looks red because there are vast amounts of rust in its soil.

511. It is absolutely silent in space.

512. Venus spins in the opposite direction than Earth, so the sunrise is in the west, and the sunset is in the east.

513. Weirdly enough, there is no mercury on the planet Mercury! Most of it is actually solid iron.

514. The footprints from the moon landings are still there.

515. If you could put Saturn in a lake, it would float.

516. The Solar and Heliospheric Observatory has found more than 2,400 comets since its launch in 1995.

517. If you could drive a car straight up, it would take you less than an hour to get to space.

That's Bonkers!

53

WHAT THE HECK IS UP THERE?

518. Radio broadcasts from Earth have now made it to over 75 star systems in our galaxy. ○

519. What planet spins faster than any other planet in the solar system? Jupiter. ○

520. Pluto used to be called a planet. Scientists decided it was too small and changed their minds. ○

521. There is an entire ring of asteroids between Mars and Jupiter. ○

522. The International Space Station orbits Earth about once every 90 minutes. ○

523. Over 25 million different things crash onto Earth from outer space every day. ○

524. Dying stars cause the biggest explosions we know of in the universe. They are called supernovae. ○

525. There is a canyon on Mars that is over ten times longer than the Grand Canyon in the United States. ○

526. Voyager 1 was launched in 1977. It left our solar system in 2012 and is probably still flying out into space. ○

527. It would take over 70,000 years for any of today's spaceships to fly to our Sun's closest star. ○

528. New evidence suggests there may have been life on Venus. Or there may still be in the upper atmosphere. ○

529. Astronomers found a planet around another star they believe is made up mostly of diamonds. ○

530. Based on the size of the planet it orbits, our Moon is the largest satellite in the solar system. ○

That's Bonkers!

STOP BUGGING ME! *Chapter 14*

531. Diseases passed by mosquito bites kill over one million people every year.

532. Scientists estimate there are 1,250,000,000 insects alive for every person. That's over 1 billion insects for every human being!

533. Many people around the world keep bugs as pets. Especially singing bugs like crickets.

534. Some insects can walk on the surface of the water without sinking.

535. It is only the female mosquitoes that bite people.

536. Did you know that it is only male crickets that chirp?

537. Did you know that Cleopatra made her lipstick from crushed ants? She used ants for the base and crushed beetles to give it the red pigment!

538. All insects have three body segments and six legs.

539. Bugs have their skeleton on the outside of their bodies.

540. Some dragonflies have over 28,000 lenses on their compound eyes.

That's Bonkers!

STOP BUGGING ME!

545. There were grasshoppers on Earth before the Dinosaurs.

541. The fastest-running bug is the Australian Tiger Beetle.

551. Hornets will hunt and eat bees.

546. Are you aware that the saliva of mosquitoes acts as an anaesthetic? This is why we usually do not notice it when a mosquito bites us.

542. Some ants are farmers, growing gardens and keeping livestock inside their nests.

552. Swarms of fireflies sometimes all flash their lights at the same time.

547. Some cicadas only come out of the about once every 15 years

543. Flies are not able to hear any sounds at all!

553. In North America, termite colonies can have over a million termites living in them.

548. Do you know what someone who studies insects is called? An entomologist.

544. Ladybugs are not bugs. Do you ever wonder why they leave yellow spots on your hand when you hold them? They bleed from their knees when they feel threatened!

554. On average, Ladybugs have a one-year lifespan.

549. An ant can lift over 20 times their own body weight, but a dung beetle can drag over 1,000 times their body weight over the ground.

555. There are more than 800 species of ants in the United States alone.

550. Bulldog ants can jump over seven other ants in one leap.

That's Bonkers!

STOP BUGGING ME!

560. One out of four insects alive is a beetle.

556. Farmers rely on insects for the food they grow.

566. Prehistoric dragonflies had wings over 2 feet long

561. Fruit flies only live for a couple of months.

557. Technically, not all insects are bugs.

567. Of all insects, the praying mantis is the only one that can turn its head.

562. A few species of ants will explode their bodies to defend the nest against attackers.

558. Did you know that some queen ants can live up to 22 years?

568. Dragonflies can fly almost as fast as cars on the freeway

563. Did you know that the bright colors on a ladybug are to warn predators to stay away?

559. The Voodoo Wasp lays its eggs inside the body of a caterpillar. After the eggs hatch and crawl out of the caterpillar's body, the caterpillar is somehow still controlled to protect the young wasps.

569. All insects hatch from eggs.

564. Gardeners often release ladybugs. The ladybugs eat aphids that destroy garden plants.

570. Most insect blood is yellow or green.

565. Honeybees have hair on their eyes!

That's Bonkers!

57

STOP BUGGING ME!

574. Honey bees use dances and wiggles to tell other bees where to find flowers.

571. Caterpillars have more individual muscles than humans.

575. Some wasps make paper out of wood. They use it to build their nests.

577. Did you know that a long time ago, pillows were made out of stones? They weren't made for comfort but to elevate people's heads so insects wouldn't crawl into their mouths while they slept.

572. You can guess the temperature by how fast crickets chirp.

576. A cockroach's head can still wiggle its antennae – even when cut off from the body.

573. All insects have antennae on their heads.

58

That's Bonkers!

Chapter 15

RIVERS, LAKES AND OCEANS

578. The Nile river in Egypt is the longest river in the world. Or is it? Recently, scientists have measured the Amazon as just a little bit longer

579. Over 96% of the water on our whole planet is in the oceans.

580. The largest island in the world is the country of Greenland.

581. The Amazon river dumps more water into the oceans than the six other biggest rivers - all put together.

582. Most of the oxygen we breathe comes from rivers, lakes, and oceans.

583. Did you know that the deepest river in the world is in Africa? The Congo river; we don't even know how deep its deepest part is yet.

584. The Dead Sea is ten times saltier than the ocean.

585. Over 65% of the water people drink comes from rivers and streams.

586. The Panama Canal is a man-made waterway created so that ships can pass between the Atlantic and Pacific oceans. The canal cuts across the narrow strip of land between North and South America.

That's Bonkers!

RIVERS, LAKES AND OCEANS

587. "The Land of a Thousand Lakes" is the country of Finland. There are over 180,000 lakes.

588. The water in the Pacific Ocean does not have as much salt as the Atlantic.

589. If there were no mountains, hills, or valleys on Earth and it was perfectly flat, it would be covered entirely in water.

590. Over 20% of all freshwater is in the Great Lakes of North America.

591. The Roe river in Montana is the shortest river in the world. It is only 2/3 the length of a football field.

592. There are over 100 million lakes on our planet.

593. The beginning of a river is called the head, but the end of the river is called the mouth.

594. The Snake River in Idaho gets its name from the shape of its path, not the animals that live along its banks.

595. There is a species of dolphin that lives in the Amazon River.

596. The Mississippi river froze over In 1899.

597. Mt Everest would be submerged entirely in Mariana's Trench - the deepest part of all the world's oceans. Mariana's Trench is the deepest part of all the world's oceans. It is so deep that Mount Everest would actually be submerged entirely in the Trench.

598. The oceans would be over 200 feet higher if all the glaciers on the planet melted.

599. More water is floating in the atmosphere than in some of the biggest lakes on the planet.

600. We have barely explored much of our oceans. Did you know that we know more about the Moon than our oceans?

60

That's Bonkers!

RIVERS, LAKES AND OCEANS

601. The Nurek Dam on the Vakhsh River is the tallest in the world. It is 984 feet at its tallest point.

602. Jellyfish Lake is a marine lagoon in the Republic of Palau in the western Pacific. It is filled with millions of golden jellyfish, and they cross the lake every day following the Sun.

603. Humans probably crossed oceans in boats before writing was invented.

604. Lake Baikal - in Russia - is the oldest and deepest lake in the world. It even has its own animal species that can't be found anywhere else.

605. The Pacific Ocean is the largest body of water on Earth.

606. The name of the Pacific Ocean means "Peaceful Sea."

607. The saltiest lake in the world is called Gaet'ale Pond. It is located in the African country of Ethiopia.

608. A river that flows into another is called a tributary.

609. Over 60% of all lakes are in the country of Canada

610. The Yangtze River in China has more ship traffic than any other river.

611. There are lakes and rivers underground in caves. We have no idea how many more exist that we have not discovered!

612. Out of all the states, Oklahoma has the most artificial lakes and has over one million surface acres of water.

613. Canada has almost three-quarters of the world's fresh water

That's Bonkers!

You're almost half way through!

All of us here at Smart Cookie Publishing hope you're enjoying the fabulous facts and we wondered if you would take just a minute to write us a review on Amazon?

Even if it's just brief we would be super excited and grateful!

Thank you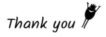

Customer Reviews

★★★★★ 15
5.0 out of 5 stars ▼

5 star ▇▇▇▇▇ 100%
4 star   0%
3 star   0%
2 star   0%
1 star   0%

Share your thoughts with othe

[Write a customer review] ◂

STRANGE BUT TRUE ANIMAL FACTS

Chapter 16

614. A hummingbird flaps its wings 80 times a second when hovering. A honey bee is faster, with 230 flaps per second.

615. Eagles can see eight times better than humans.

616. The heart is in the head of shrimp - not in their bodies.

617. Did you know that Chameleons can move their eyes in different directions?

618. Some animals can regrow body parts if they lose them.

619. A hummingbird's nest is about the size of a walnut.

620. Cows have best friends and get lonely and depressed if they are separated from each other.

621. The average life expectancy of a pelican in the wild is around 20 years.

622. After mating, male octopi wander off to die. The females can lay up to 400,000 eggs and will obsessively guard and protect them at any cost.

623. Did you know that most elephants weigh less than the tongue of a blue whale?

That's Bonkers!

STRANGE BUT TRUE ANIMAL FACTS

624. Woodpeckers' tongues wrap around their brain to cushion them from a concussion when they peck against tree trunks.

625. Butterflies taste their food with their feet. Well, that's not strange at all!

626. Cats have three eyelids, but one is usually hidden under the two on the outside.

627. Did you know that Sloths can hold their breath longer than dolphins can?

628. The closest living relative to a hippo is a whale!

629. Hippos make sounds with their vocal cords, but these sounds come out of their nostrils.

630. Cows don't sleep standing up - that's a myth! They can doze off but have to lie down to really sleep.

631. Bats are the main pollinators of the agave plant. Without them, we wouldn't have delicious agave syrup.

632. Did you know that horses can't breathe through their mouths? They can only breathe through their nose.

633. The pupil in a goat's eye is rectangular!

634. Did you know that a chameleon's tongue can be twice as long as its entire body?

635. Some species of spiders look like ants, an excellent way for them to catch an unsuspecting ant for lunch.

636. Hippos close their ears when they are underwater. They hear through their jaw bones.

637. Did you know that over 100 people are killed by elephants each year in India?

64

That's Bonkers!

STRANGE BUT TRUE ANIMAL FACTS

645. Cockroaches can live up to a whole week without a head.

638. At birth, baby kangaroos, known as "joeys," weigh only 2 grams (around the size of a jelly bean).

646. When an animal is poisonous, it is because eating it or touching it can make you sick. Toads are poisonous.

639. An octopus has nine brains. They must be brilliant!

647. When an animal is venomous, it is because being bitten or injected makes you sick. Some snakes and some spiders are venomous.

640. Squirrels warn each other about danger by twitching their tails.

648. King Cobra venom can kill an adult in less than an hour.

641. Archerfish catch bugs to eat by spitting at them to knock them into the water.

649. An electric eel can generate over 800 volts of electricity. It would take over 530 flashlight batteries to do that.

642. Contrary to popular belief, camels do not store water in their humps; they actually store fat tissue.

650. Cows that are given names and one-on-one attention will produce more milk.

643. Many birds can sleep with one eye open.

651. Did you know that the lion's roar can be heard up to 5 miles away?`

644. You can estimate the age of a horse by looking at its teeth.

That's Bonkers!

65

STRANGE BUT TRUE ANIMAL FACTS

652. Did you know that most kangaroos are left-handed?

653. Some tarantulas can go over two years without eating.

654. If a dolphin mother stops swimming, her newborn will sink. For the first few weeks of life, young dolphins don't have enough fat to float.

655. A hippo can easily hold an entire pumpkin in its mouth. They could beat you in a foot race too!

656. A giraffe has the same number of bones in their neck as you do in your whole body!

657. Jonathan, the tortoise, is the oldest animal alive. It is estimated that he is around 193 years old.

658. Koala bears have unique fingerprints, just like humans.

659. The amount of poop from an elephant in one day would weigh more than two human adults put together.

660. There is a lizard that squirts blood out of its eyes to scare off predators.

661. All earthworms are both male and female.

662. Dolphins sleep with one eye open.

663. One out of every ten bones in a cat is in its tail.

664. Porcupine quills are hollow, which makes them float. It is like they are wearing a natural life preserver.

665. Moles use their mouths to help dig their tunnels.

66

That's Bonkers!

STRANGE BUT TRUE ANIMAL FACTS

672. Elephants can't jump. They are the only animal with legs that can't.

666. Frogs don't throw up. If they have eaten something they shouldn't have, they push out their entire stomach, clean it with their front feet and then swallow it again! This action is called full gastric eversion - something cool to watch on YouTube.

673. Did you know that an elephant's trunk is also called a proboscis? Cool name, don't you think?

674. Hummingbirds are like little helicopters. They can hover and fly in all directions - even backward!

667. A group of kangaroos is called a "mob."

675. A single bite from the King Cobra can release enough venom to kill up to 20 people.

668. Some snails have strong enough venom that they could kill a human!

676. Pigs are clean animals and don't sweat as they do not have sweat glands.

669. Did you know that pigs are more intelligent than dogs?

677. Pigs roll in mud to cool down their body temperature.

670. Dolphins only sleep on one side of their brain at a time; the other half stays alert so that the dolphin can still go to the surface to breathe and to look for predators.

678. You can find bees on every single continent except Antarctica.

671. Believe it or not, avocados are poisonous to birds!

679. Many frogs eat their skin after shedding it.

That's Bonkers!

STRANGE BUT TRUE ANIMAL FACTS

680. Brand new baby pandas are the size of a mouse!

681. A group of butterflies is called a "kaleidoscope?"

682. Dogs fake sneeze to signal that they want to play with us or simply get our attention.

683. Elephants can swim for up to 6 hours and even swim underwater.

684. There are no black panthers. This species does not exist! What we mistake for black panthers are either black leopards or black jaguars.

685. Did you know that squirrel's teeth grow 5 inches a year?

686. Contrary to what most people think of lemurs, they do not suspend from their tails.

687. Some dogs have been trained to detect disease in people by smell.

688. Researchers do not know why but male mice are scared of the smell of bananas.

689. Did you know that a group of porcupines is called a "prickle"?

690. Did you know that a water animal called an axolotl can regenerate its heart or limbs if they are damaged?

691. Orca whales can sometimes be very aggressive and attack boats.

692. A single porcupine can have up to 30,000 quills.

693. Honeybees have very tiny hair on their eyes to help them collect pollen.

694. An adult panda can spend between 10-12 hours a day eating. That is because they need to eat at least 28 pounds of bamboo every day!

695. Most pelicans have air sacs in their bones. These sacs protect them when they dive into the water from high in the sky and keep them lighter as they can fly to 10,000 feet.

That's Bonkers!

YOU WON'T BELIEVE YOUR EYES

Chapter 17

696. Hawks and eagles can see eight times better than us.

697. The colored part of the eye is called the iris.

698. Most of what you learn comes from your eyes.

699. The most active muscles in your body are in your eyes.

700. Our eyes can only detect three different colors - red, green, or blue. All the colors of the rainbow are a mix of those three colors.

701. Did you know that owls are the only bird that lowers their upper eyelid to blink? All the other birds raise their lower eyelid to blink.

702. If you want to see a dim object like a star, look slightly away from it. The side - or periphery - of our vision is more sensitive to light but can't make out details as well.

703. Horses have almost a 360-degree field of vision.

704. Our eyes have 256 unique traits instead of just 40 with our fingerprints. No kidding retinal scans are used so much in movies.

That's Bonkers!

YOU WON'T BELIEVE YOUR EYES

705. Wolves have round pupils like us, but foxes have slits more like a cat.

706. Most of your eye is filled with a clear jelly-like fluid called Vitreous Humor

707. Did you know that the spots of light you see after rubbing your eyes are called phosphenes?

708. Your eyes are the most complex organ in your body except your brain.

709. Violet is the rarest eye color.

710. People can have two different colored eyes. Some can even have two different colors in one eye.

711. When someone does have two different colored eyes, it is called Heterochromia.

712. Skunks typically try to aim for the eyes of their attackers when they spray.

713. Owls do not have eyeballs, so they can't move their eyes!

714. The cornea is the only part of your body without blood vessels.

715. Babies see things in black and white for the first few weeks they are alive.

716. Most people can read a piece of paper faster than a computer screen.

70

That's Bonkers!

YOU WON'T BELIEVE YOUR EYES

717. Two parents with blue eyes can only have blue-eyed children.

718. Your eyes have over 2 million different parts. Most of them are on the back of the eye.

719. The front of your eye works exactly like eyeglass lenses.

720. Owls can see the color blue, but no other birds can.

721. Your eyes can recognize about 10 million different colors.

722. The black part in the center of your eye is called the pupil. It gets bigger and smaller to control the amount of light you see.

723. Most people's eyes weigh less than an ounce

724. Our eyes focus on about 50 different things every second.

725. Sailors used to think that wearing a gold earring would improve eyesight.

726. Your eye reaches its full size by the time you are 12.

727. Giant Squids have the largest eye of any living animal. They are bigger than a dinner plate.

728. Shark corneas have been used on people to help them see.

That's Bonkers!

YOU WON'T BELIEVE YOUR EYES

729. More boys are color-blind than girls.

730. Every person with blue eyes shares a common ancestor that lived about 10,000 years ago.

731. Sea stars have eyes. Unlike humans, sea stars have an eye on the tip of each of their arms. The eye does not have great vision like our eye, but it can detect light and dark.

That's Bonkers!

COULD YOU HAVE SURVIVED IN PREHISTORIC TIMES?
Chapter 18

732. Prehistoric people had to carry everything they owned with them wherever they went.

733. There were birds large enough to eat small prehistoric children. Scientists have found at least one skeleton that happened to be in Africa.

734. Humans have been on Earth for 2 million years, but dinosaurs lasted 150 million years before becoming extinct.

735. Prehistoric children didn't have doors to lock or covers to hide under. But they also didn't have closets for monsters to hide in either.

736. The stone age lasted for over 2 million years.

737. Everything prehistoric people needed was made from plants, animals, or rocks until the end of the stone age.

738. Before lighters and matches, a fire had to be carried from place to place. It also had to be created by smacking two special rocks together.

That's Bonkers!

COULD YOU HAVE SURVIVED IN PREHISTORIC TIMES?

739. Prehistoric houses were often animal hides over stick frames

740. People in pre-historic times didn't stay in one place for very long. They constantly moved in search of food.

741. People proba-bly didn't have any shoes for most of the prehistoric era.

742. Africa was still attached to Europe at the start of the Stone age.

743. People used to have to kill animals to get furs to keep warm.

744. Prehistoric people had to face giant cave bears, giant sloths, and giant hyenas, among other predators that wanted to eat them.

745. Prehistor-ic people did hunt. But they were likely scavengers more than active hunters.

746. The first bow and arrow showed up about 12,000–10,000 years ago.

747. Scientists think that goose-bumps may be a leftover from when we were hairier in prehis-toric times. It is possible that we puffed up our fur to look bigger, just like house cats do today.

748. Humans started turning wild wolves into pet dogs in the stone age.

749. By the end of the Stone Age, people had started farming, which led to settling down in cities.

750. We call it the stone age because that is when we started making tools, most of which were stone.

751. There was no writing in prehistoric times.

752. Many prehistoric people lived as long as we do today.

74

That's Bonkers!

COULD YOU HAVE SURVIVED IN PREHISTORIC TIMES?

753. Our prehistoric ancestors may have eaten more bone marrow than actual meat. But that couldn't have happened without hunting live animals.

754. Humans almost went extinct during the stone age. Some scientists believe there may have been as few as a couple of hundred on the whole planet. There are probably more than that in your school.

755. There were several different species of human-like creatures alive in prehistoric times.

756. Our DNA tells us that every single person alive today can trace their history back to one single female that lived about 150,000 years ago.

757. Life for prehistoric humans was like camping every single day.

758. Prehistoric people generally lived in small groups and tribes.

759. There were four primary ice ages during the Stone Age.

760. All the languages in the world likely came from a single group of simple sounds.

761. The Stone Age's end was about the same as the end of the last Ice Age.

762. The Bronze Age started when humans learned how to work with metal. This marked the end of prehistoric times and the start of modern times.

763. Most people today have traces of Neanderthals in their DNA.

That's Bonkers!

That's Bonkers!

Chapter 19

THINGS YOUR PARENTS DON'T EVEN KNOW (ASK THEM AND YOU'LL SEE...)

764. Even dolls have lives. Barbie's real name is Barbara Millicent Roberts.

765. Bananas don't grow on trees! They are the berries of an herb plant. Yes, you read that right - a banana is a berry, not a fruit.

766. The first Spanish settlement in North America was built with wood from Christopher Columbus's wrecked ship, the Santa Maria.

767. Google rented goats to mow the lawn at their company headquarters.

768. Rats laugh when tickled. They just do it at too high a pitch for us to hear.

769. Parts of ships at sea often glow on their own from static electricity.

769. Did you know that Mall of America doesn't have heating even though it's located in Minnesota? During the winter, the heat produced by the lights and the heat from the shoppers is enough to keep the mall warm.

771. An 11-year-old boy invented Popsicles!

That's Bonkers!

THINGS YOUR PARENTS DON'T EVEN KNOW
(ASK THEM AND YOU'LL SEE...)

772. All polar bears are left-handed.

773. Kangaroos can not walk backward.

774. Ask your parents if they know at what speed Heinz Ketchup travels leaving the bottle - answer: it travels at 0.028 miles per hour.

775. Regular farmyard chickens communicate using 24 different sounds.

776. Chipotle and jalapeño are two different names for the same pepper.

777. About 5 percent of the crust of the Earth is iron.

778. Tanks in the British military are set up to make tea at tea time.

779. Cows can not walk downstairs. But they can walk up.

780. When they are first born, a giraffe is as tall as a full-grown adult.

781. One poor person had hiccups for 69 years straight.

782. Did you know that the modern-day iPhone has more processing power than NASA's entire computer setup for the first moon landing mission?

783. Bees have been around since the dinosaurs.

784. The Empire State Building has its own zip code assigned by the United States Postal Service.

785. Rhubarb and asparagus are the only vegetables that don't need to be replanted every year.

786. It can take 450-500 years for a plastic bottle to decompose.

78   That's Bonkers!

THINGS YOUR PARENTS DON'T EVEN KNOW
(ASK THEM AND YOU'LL SEE...)

787. A thundercloud forms over the Tiwi Islands in Australia at approximately 3pm almost every single day.

788. You can't hum while you are holding your nose closed.

789. The average person spends two entire years of their life on the phone.

790. It is illegal to ride a bike in Illinois without your hands on the handlebars or feet on the pedals.

791. Believe it or not, some people have a fear of getting haircuts, and the name for that fear is Tonsurephobia.

792. 12% of people dream entirely in black and white.

793. More people are killed by donkeys every year than in plane crashes.

794. If you see a military statue of a man on a horse and the horse has his two front legs up in the air, it means that the man died in battle.

795. There are 118 ridges on the edge of a United States dime.

796. Only about 7% of the people on Earth are left-handed.

797. Wolves have been tracked traveling over 1,000 miles from their starting point.

798. As far as doctors and scientists know, sharks and rays never get cancer.

799. The rainiest place on Earth is Mount Wai'ale'ale in Hawaii.

800. Everybody knows recycling is great, but did you know that recycling one aluminium can save enough energy to run a 55-inch HDTV for a movie?

That's Bonkers!

THINGS YOUR PARENTS DON'T EVEN KNOW
(ASK THEM AND YOU'LL SEE...)

801. President Abraham Lincoln was a champion wrestler with only one loss.

802. If the US recycled all of its aluminium cans, the energy saved from it could power 4.1 million homes for an entire year!

803. A can of diet soda will float in water, but regular soda will sink.

804. More garlic is grown in China than in any other country in the world.

805. There are more people in the world named Mohammad than any other name.

806. Door knobs made of brass or copper can disinfect themselves in about 8 hours.

807. A woman was elected to the United States Congress before women had the right to vote.

808. A golf ball has 366 dimples.

809. Did you know that there are 293 different ways to make change for a US dollar?

810. Every day, roughly 82 YEARS' worth of videos are published on YouTube!

811. Hippo milk is pink. That's right, pink!

812. Fortune cookies aren't Chinese! They were actually invented in America and are seen in China as an American symbol.

813. The extreme fear of having to cook is called: Mageirocophobia.

814. The calendars in Ethiopia are 7 to 8 years behind ours, so if you read this fact in 2023, it is the year 2015 for them!

815. Ask your parents if they know the name of the skin on a turkey's beak - answer: it is called a snood.

816. People with red hair account for only two percent of the world's population.

That's Bonkers!

Fantastic Natural Phenomena
Chapter 20

817. The oldest trees in the world are about 5,000 years old.

818. There is a thunderstorm somewhere on Earth every single minute.

819. There is a beach in Hawaii with green sand. I bet you know what the name of the beach is...

820. A waterfall in Antarctica makes it look like the glacier is bleeding. The water is so full of iron that it rusts when it hits the air – this is where it gets its color.

821. There are over 30 species of mushrooms that glow in the dark. This chemical reaction is called bioluminescence, and people have been known to use these mushrooms to light their way through the woods.

822. Did you know that a lunar eclipse is the shadow of the Earth on the moon?

823. Some tornadoes can have winds of up to 300 miles per hour.

824. Over 44 million red crabs go to Christmas Island in Australia every fall to lay eggs.

That's Bonkers!

FANTASTIC NATURAL PHENOMENA

825. In the fall, when leaves change colors, they become their actual color. In the summer, chlorophyll makes them turn green and hide their true colors.

826. The world's tallest tree measures more than 360 feet. It is a coast redwood and is located in California. The tree is only a few feet shorter than the Empire State Building!

827. The moonflower only blooms at night when the moon is out. Its name makes a lot of sense!

828. Dolphins and bats both make sounds to know what is around them. They listen to the echoes of their sounds to understand where objects are and their shape. They can "see" with their ears.

829. A tree can filter up to 60 pounds of pollutants from the air around us each year!

830. A rainbow is caused by sunlight passing through raindrops.

831. The Kawah Ijen volcano in Indonesia glows blue at night!

832. Fire tornadoes can form in extremely hot forest fires.

833. A tsunami is almost unnoticeable out at sea. It only becomes a huge wave when it enters shallow water.

834. There is a single fungus in Oregon that is over 2,000 acres in size. Some scientists say it is the largest living thing on the planet.

835. Did you know that a bolt of lightning is hotter than the sun?

836. A lightning bolt strikes so quickly that it can circle the Earth eight times in just one second.

That's Bonkers!

FANTASTIC NATURAL PHENOMENA

837. Under the right conditions, a bright green flash can be seen at sunset. It has no name and is referred to as an optical phenomenon.

838. Ships at sea often give off visible light caused by static electricity. It is called St. Elmo's Fire.

839. Salmon lay their eggs in the same spot in a river where they hatched. After spending several years swimming around in the ocean, they can find the right place.

840. The biggest hailstone ever recorded was almost as wide as a soccer ball.

841. Okunoshima island, located in the inland sea of Japan, 43 miles east of the city of Hiroshima, is only inhabited by bunnies.

842. The ground is exploding in Russia! Well, just certain spots in Siberia where methane gas has heated up under the permafrost and then exploded under the pressure.

843. Did you know that of all of the natural disasters declared by the US president, 90% of them involved flooding?

844. The state of Maine in the United States is the closest State to Africa.

845. When volcanoes erupt, lightning is often seen in the erupting cloud.

846. A lake in Canada is famous for gas bubbles that get trapped in ice as it freezes. The bubbles can be seen from the surface of the lake.

847. There are over 2,000 tornadoes on Earth every year.

848. A landslide in Alaska caused a tsunami as tall as a 150-story building. It was the largest tsunami known to man. It was over ten times larger than most of those caused by earthquakes.

849. The rocks scattered in the desert of Death Valley, California, seem to move across the desert floor by themselves. Scientists are not exactly sure how it happens.

That's Bonkers!

FANTASTIC NATURAL PHENOMENA

850. When there are two full moons in one month, it is called a Blue Moon. This usually only happens once every 2 or 3 years.

851. One United States park ranger has been struck by lightning seven different times in his life. He survived all of them.

852. Ball lightning was thought to be a myth until a few scientists witnessed it happening from an airplane they were flying in.

853. Waterspouts are like a tornado that forms over a large lake or ocean, carrying water with fast swirling winds.

854. Fungus in the forest soil help to pass messages between trees.

855. Some beaches can be seen to glow at night. It is caused by tiny sea creatures that give off light, like fireflies and glowworms.

856. Waves in the ocean sometimes combine to create rogue waves up to 10 times as tall as nearby waves.

857. The sun can make rainbows, but the moon can also make moonbows at night.

858. There are an average of 6,000 lightning strikes per minute on this planet.

859. You can't see it, but plants move slowly to follow the sun.

860. About twice a year, there is a blood moon. During the blood moon, the moon will look red from some places on Earth.

861. The largest landslide ever recorded was in 1980 in Washington State. It was triggered by the eruption of Mt St Helens.

862. Hawaii moves four inches toward Japan every year.

That's Bonkers!

UNEXPLAINED MYSTERIES
Chapter 21

863. We don't know for sure if King Arthur was a real person. Or not!

864. Sasquatch is the Native American name for Bigfoot.

865. The pyramids are built with blocks of stone that our most powerful machines would have trouble moving today

866. A bridge in Scotland seems to make dogs jump off. Over 50 dogs have died, and hundreds of others have been injured, jumping off the Overtoun bridge for no apparent reason.

867. A beast called The Chupacabra has been reported to hunt livestock throughout the Central Americas. Its name means "goat-sucker."

868. There are huge drawings on the Earth all over the planet made by prehistoric people. They can only be seen from an airplane.

869. A radio telescope picked up a signal in 1977 that may have been from aliens. It is called The WOW Signal.

867. Easter Island has enormous stone carvings of heads. No one knows how they were made or how they were moved to that location.

That's Bonkers!

UNEXPLAINED MYSTERIES

871. There are huge cats in Australia that are the size of mountain lions. After DNA testing, researchers discovered that they are just feral cats. No one knows how they have grown so big.

872. The man known as DB Cooper jumped out of a hijacked passenger jet somewhere between Seattle and Las Vegas with several bags of ransom money. He has never been found.

873. The American sailing ship Mary Celeste was discovered abandoned in the Atlantic Ocean in 1872. The cargo was still there, and there was no damage to the ship. All that was missing was a single lifeboat. No one from the crew was ever heard from again.

874. According to physics, knowing what happens inside a black hole is impossible. We can only make the best guess.

875. A person or group going by the name of Cicada 3301 has been leaving hidden puzzles all over the world. Some in real life, some on the internet. Why they are doing it is unknown.

876. Many skulls made of clear, glass-like crystals have been found all over South America. They are believed to be thousands of years old. No one knows how or why they were made.

877. 5.2 million people worldwide helped use the computer software SETI @ Home to search for broadcasts from aliens in space.

878. A star known as Przybylski's Star has elements in its upper atmosphere that modern physics tells us should be exceedingly rare. No other star like it has been found, leading some to suspect aliens might be the cause.

86

That's Bonkers!

UNEXPLAINED MYSTERIES

879. Two children wandered out of the woods in medieval England. They spoke a language that no one recognized and had green skin. No one knows where they are from or how their skin got that color.

880. The Loch Ness Monster is a giant "sea serpent" type creature. There have been sightings reported of the Loch Ness Monster in Scotland for over 1,500 years. It remains a mystery today.

881. 25 Americans working in Cuba got sick near the same time. They all blamed it on a sound they heard. The cause has not yet been explained.

882. No one knows how or why stone age humans created Stonehenge.

883. A book called the Voynich manuscript is written in a language or code that no one can figure out. It seems to be hundreds of years old. Where it came from and what it says is still unknown.

884. Malaysian Airlines flight 370 disappeared with 239 passengers over the Indian Ocean. The most extensive search in aviation history was unable to find the wreckage.

885. Someone once buried something over 90 feet underground on Oak Island, Nova Scotia, Canada. A booby trap flooded the hole and prevented further digging at that time. There is a long-running show on television about it, but no one really knows how the hole got there or why.

886. 200 ancient Roman jars were found underwater in a bay in Brazil. As far as we know, Romans never made it to that side of the world. How did they get there?

887. Doctors have no idea why some kids suffer from growing pains.

That's Bonkers!

87

That's Bonkers!

YOU HAD NO CLUE THIS HAPPENED

Chapter 22

888. 30 United States House of Representatives members got into an actual fistfight in 1858 while debating official government business.

890. A woman that survived the sinking of the Titanic also survived two other ship disasters. All three ships were run by the same company - the White Star Line.

892. In 2010, a massive traffic jam in Beijing, China, lasted over nine days. I will travel on my bicycle if I ever visit Beijing.

893. Did you know that John Fairfax became the first person to row by himself across an ocean on the same day man first landed on the moon?

889. Writers C.S. Lewis and Aldous Huxley both died on the same day; most people didn't know because it was the same day US President John F Kennedy died.

891. After one battle of the American Civil War, some of the soldiers noticed that their wounds were glowing. To make it even stranger, those that glowed seemed to heal better than those that didn't.

894. Pope Gregory IV ordered the extermination of all black cats throughout Europe.

That's Bonkers!

YOU HAD NO CLUE THIS HAPPENED

895. Over 7,000 Germans tried to establish a German settlement in what is now the state of Texas.

899. A single full-grown tree pumps out enough oxygen to keep up to 20 people alive each and every day.

896. A tsunami wave can travel faster than a jet airplane.

900. Adolf Hitler was nominated for the Nobel Peace Prize.

903. In 1876, numerous small chunks of meat seemed to rain out of the sky over a Kentucky farm. No one is quite sure exactly how this happened.

897. An Englishman wrote the music for the Star Spangled Banner.

901. April 22, 1970, was the first Earth Day.

898. In 1922, people rioted against the fashion tradition of switching from straw to felt hats in mid-September.

902. A flight attendant survived a fall from over 30,000 feet without a parachute.

904. A tank full of molasses in Boston burst, releasing a flood of sticky syrup on the streets. The flood was so big 21 people were killed!

90

That's Bonkers!

Chapter 23

FOOD FOR THOUGHT

905. Neither a tomato nor an avocado is a vegetable. Each one is a fruit.

908. Peanuts are actually a bean, not a nut.

911. Three Musketeers candy bars used to come in 3 different flavors. That's how they got the name.

906. Did you know that the first ice cream recipe was found in a recipe book from 1665?

909. Pistachios, like peanuts, are also not a nut. Pistachios are a fruit.

912. Both pineapples and strawberries are actually called Multiple Fruit. A pineapple is a collection of many berries, and a strawberry is a collection of many fruits.

907. Some cultures eat the meat of dogs the way others eat steak from cows.

910. Honey never spoils. In fact, it is the only food that doesn't!

That's Bonkers!

FOOD FOR THOUGHT

913. According to legend, the sandwich was invented when a guy playing cards asked for a slice of roast beef. He asked for it to be put in two slices of bread to let him eat with his hands and not leave the game. That must have been an excellent game of cards!

914. White chocolate isn't chocolate at all. But it still tastes good.

915. Believe it or not, in 2001, Belgium launched a program to replace sugary drinks and soda in school lunches with beer!

916. If you eat enough carrots, you can make your skin turn orange.

917. The first big customer of M&M candies was the United States Army.

918. People perceive that candy or drinks that are colored red taste sweeter.

919. Humans need 14 different vitamins and 13 different minerals from their food to survive.

920. The average number of licks needed to eat a scoop of ice cream is 50.

921. You can buy Coca-Cola in every country except Cuba and North Korea.

922. Fresh garlic can be absorbed through the soles of your feet, and you'll end up tasting it in your mouth.

923. Temperature can affect people's appetite, and a cold person will likely eat more food.

924. The holes in cheeses like Swiss cheese are called eyes. Swiss cheese without eyes is said to be blind - seriously!

925. A bad egg will float in a glass of cold water.

926. Peas are the oldest vegetable cultivated by humankind.

92

That's Bonkers!

FOOD FOR THOUGHT

927. Almonds are a seed and are related to peaches. They are like a peach pit without the peach.

928. Strawberries have their seeds on the outside. They are the only fruit that does.

929. Some of the strangest flavors of ice cream are avocado, garlic, chilli, licorice, Stilton cheese, and bacon!

930. 98% of houses in the United States will buy ice cream at some point this year.

931. Some people dip their french fries in mayonnaise instead of ketchup. (I am one of them!)

932. Processed hamburger meat in a fast food burger can have the meat of 50-100 different cows in it.

933. The different colors of Froot Loops cereal all taste exactly the same!

934. Did you know that goat meat is the most popular in the world, not cow meat?

935. About 40% of the food prepared in the United States is thrown away.

936. Hawaiian pizza came from Canada, not Hawaii.

937. The spiciness in hot foods like peppers is from a chemical called capsaicin.

938. Believe it or not, chocolate ice cream was invented before vanilla ice cream.

939. 25% of the world's hazelnuts are used to make the famous Nutella spread.

940. Did you know that a dentist invented cotton candy?

941. People in the United States eat more tomatoes than any other fruit or vegetable.

That's Bonkers!

FOOD FOR THOUGHT

942. Car wax, believe it or not, is used to polish some of the fruits we buy at the grocery stores to make them shiny.

943. The holes in saltine crackers are there to prevent them from blowing up like a balloon while baking.

944. One man ate 63 hotdogs in 10 minutes.

945. Jack-o-lanterns were originally carved inside potatoes. The English also used beets.

946. The delicious filling of a Kit Kat chocolate bar is made from the crumbs of broken Kit Kat bars. What a brilliant way to recycle!

947. Did you know that cheese is the most stolen food in the world?

948. There is more sugar in lemons than in strawberries.

949. Did you know that McDonald's serves spaghetti in the Philippines?

950. It can sometimes take 2 or 3 years for a pineapple plant to produce fruit.

951. Most wasabi paste isn't made from real wasabi. It is made from horseradish.

952. Potatoes have been grown in space.

953. One of the ingredients in Mountain Dew is orange juice.

954. Many fruits belong to the rose family: Raspberries, strawberries, peaches, apples, plumbs, pears, apricots, and cherries.

955. The most enormous squash ever grown belonged to Joel Jarvis from Port Elgin, Ontario, Canada. His monster squash weighed 1,487 pounds!

 94

That's Bonkers!

FOOD FOR THOUGHT

956. Cashews grow on cashew apples.

957. French fries were invented in Belgium - not France.

958. A very common red food dye is made from crushed beetles. Yup - the insects.

959. Most people know white cauliflower, but there are also purple, green, and orange varieties.

960. Australians eat the most meat per person in the world. People in India eat the least.

961. There were noodles found in China that were over 4,000 years old.

962. Before the 18th century, it was considered a bad thing by the church to use forks.

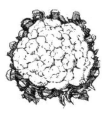

963. Every single day, Americans eat the equivalent of eighteen acres of pizza. That's almost 14 football fields of pizza! WOW!

964. In Sweden, banana topping on pizza is very popular.

965. The average American eats approximately 200 sandwiches per year.

966. Europeans thought tomatoes were poisonous until the 1800s.

967. The average number of sesame seeds on a McDonald's Big Mac bun is 178

That's Bonkers!

96   *That's Bonkers!*

Chapter 24

WATCH YOUR TONGUE

968. There are over 170,000 different words in the English language.

969. You can say "Hong Kong" without moving your lips! That would make you a ventriloquist.

970. Today, we add about 4,000 new words to the English language every year. Only nine were dropped in the year 2021

971. Did you know that the Scots language has over 400 words for "snow"?

972. The oldest language that people still speak is called Tamil. It is over 5,000 years old.

973. 67 out of 195 countries use English as their official language - more than any other language. French is the second most used language.

974. There are only 40 different sounds used in the English language. The native Hawaiian language has the fewest: Only 18.

975. Did you know that in the English language, the letter 'e' is the most common?

976. Written Chinese characters are not letters like English. Instead, they are pictographs that represent words or ideas. Egyptian hieroglyphs work the same way.

977. Most English-speaking people agree that the toughest tongue twister is: "sixth sick sheik's sixth sheep's sick."

That's Bonkers!

WATCH YOUR TONGUE

978. NASA astronauts are required to learn Russian.

979. The letter J wasn't invented until 1630. I wonder what they used before.

980. Modern English is the third version of the English language. Before that came Old English and Middle English. We probably couldn't understand someone speaking Old English at all today.

981. Many of us remember the English vowels as a, e, i, o, u, and sometimes y. But the letter 'w' can sometimes be a vowel too.

982. A duel is between two people. Truel is an actual word for a fight involving three people.

983. There are over 50,000 symbols in traditional Chinese writing.

984. The plural of Goose is Geese, and the plural of Moose is still Moose because the word Goose comes from Latin while Moose comes from Native American languages, so it doesn't follow the same rules as most other words.

985. Russian has no word for "is" or "am." But it does have words for "was" and "will be."

986. The Korean language is not related to any other language still spoken.

987. Before the Guinness Book of World Records was around, some people reportedly could read or speak hundreds of languages.

988. In parts of England, some people routinely talk in rhyming slang. They may say, "my plates of meat hurt," but they mean, "my feet hurt." They call it Cockney Rhyming Slang.

你好

98

That's Bonkers!

WATCH YOUR TONGUE

989. Weirdly enough, the word synonym does not have a synonym!

990. People in Papua New Guinea speak over 800 different languages.

991. The word 'alphabet' comes from the names of the first letters of the Greek alphabet: alpha and beta.

992. More people in China can speak English than in the United States.

993. The word 'polymath' means someone that knows about many different subjects. Mathematics does not have to be one of them.

994. A person that is afraid of eggs is called an Ovophobe.

995. Did you know that Bolivia has 37 official languages?

996. The words NOON and SWIMS can be flipped backward and upside down and still be spelled the same way!

997. Japanese is the fastest-spoken language in the world.

998. More than 50% of the world's population can speak more than one language.

999. Did you know that Russian was the first language spoken in outer space? ПРИВЕТ

1000. A person that speaks many different languages is called a polyglot.

1001. The most extensive alphabet of any language on Earth is 74. The shortest is 12.

1002. People that use American Sign Language cannot always understand people that use British Sign Language, even though the countries both speak English.

1003. When kids first learn to talk, they can learn over ten new words daily.

That's Bonkers!

WATCH YOUR TONGUE

1004. You can't think of a word that rhymes with 'orange.'

1005. The United States never declared an official language.

1006. There are at least 24 recognizable dialects of English spoken in the United States.

1007. The word "school" comes from the ancient Greek for "free time."

1008. Many people have been observed talking to themselves in sign language, exactly how someone may speak out loud while thinking.

1009. The word 'set' has more different meanings than any other word in the English language.

1010. About 1/5 of the people on the planet speak some form of Chinese.

1011. The English language got its start in what is now Germany - not in England.

1012. You can do something once or twice. But if you do it one more time, you've done it thrice.

1013. The official language of the sky is English - all pilots and air traffic controllers have to speak English.

1014. Did you know that Nigeria has more English speakers than the UK? There are approximately 90 million English speakers in Nigeria compared to 60 million in the UK.

1015. 'Dreamt' is the only common English word that ends with the letters' mt.'

1016. Q is the only letter that doesn't appear in the name of any of the US states.

1018. Did you know that you cannot say B or M without both your lips touching?

1017. Weird does not follow the i before e rule - that is so weird!

你好

That's Bonkers!

HACKS, TIPS AND TRICKS
Chapter 26

1019. You can freeze chewing gum with an ice cube to get it out of your hair or clothes.

1020. A cornstarch and water mixture will pour like water but stay solid if you try to splash it. It is similar to Silly Putty. Both are considered non-Newtonian fluids.

1021. A crumbling cake isn't pleasant, but you can avoid it and serve a perfectly cut slice of cake by using a long piece of unflavored dental floss to slice through it.

1022. Clear fingernail polish can be used to waterproof things.

1023. Fill an old box with toilet paper rolls and use it to store rolled-up cords.

1024. The sticky part of PostIt notes does a great job of getting dust and dirt off a computer keyboard.

1025. You can push a straw through the bottom of a strawberry to get the green leafy part off the top.

That's Bonkers!

HACKS, TIPS AND TRICKS

1026. You can carve your own stamp out of a raw potato.

1027. A clothes hanger is a great way to store necklaces that would otherwise get all tangled together.

1028. Make a hole in the middle of your plate of leftovers to make them heat up more evenly in the microwave.

1029. Poke the handle of your popsicle through a paper cupcake cup to keep the melting popsicle from getting all over your hand.

1030. If your paint brushes get all messy looking, you can get them back to a sharp point by twirling them against a wet bar of soap and then letting them dry.

1031. If you refrigerate your rubber bands, they will last longer.

1032. If you place your smartphone into a bowl, its concave shape will act as a speaker for you and make everything coming out of your phone much louder.

1033. You can make a collar for your dog or cat out of the collar of an old button-up shirt.

1034. Did you know that you can use the inside of a banana peel to polish leather shoes and silverware?

1035. You can also use the inside of a banana peel to rub on your skin and stop mosquito bites from itching!

That's Bonkers!

HACKS, TIPS AND TRICKS

1036. Toothpaste can often get scratches out of soft metal or plastic.

1037. Use lego bricks to make pen holders. You can also use the containers you'll make to hold other things like loose change, hair pins, toothbrushes, etc.

1038. If you forget or lose your adaptor for your charger and can no longer plug it into an electrical outlet, then plug it into the USB port on a TV.

1039. If you have a few different keys and sometimes forget which one is for what, you can easily fix this problem by painting the bow of each key with a different nail polish color.

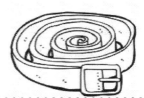

1040. If your backpack rips and you have books to carry, you can use your belt to strap them together. It makes them easier to carry.

That's Bonkers!

That's Bonkers!

ZOOM, ZOOM, ZOOM!

Chapter 26

1041. The fastest car driven was powered by two jet engines

1042. The biggest engine in the world produces over 100,000 horsepower. That's the same power as more than 500 cars.

1043. Most modern car engines spin 2,000-4,000 times every minute while driving.

1044. Over 150,000 new cars are made every day.

1045. A motor powers electric cars; to be an engine, it has to burn fuel.

1046. The very first electric car in the United States was back in 1890.

1047. The name Volkswagen means "The People's Car."

1048. The most powerful engines we know how to make are rocket engines.

1049. There are over 30,000 parts in most modern cars. Only about 200-300 of those are in the engine.

1050. Trains used to be powered by the steam of boiling water.

That's Bonkers!

ZOOM, ZOOM, ZOOM!

1051. Up to 1894, motorcycles were called "Petrol Cycles."

1052. You can build a working rocket engine with no moving parts at all.

1053. A modern car is powered down the road with 6,000 – 12,000 tiny explosions every minute.

1054. High-speed trains can travel at speeds up to 361 mph. Japan, France, China, and Germany currently have them, and the United States has plans to build one.

1055. Robbie Madison had the world record for the longest motorcycle jump of 328 feet and 10 inches; that's the length of more than 11 school buses!

1056. The first gasoline engines were used to pump water more often than anything else.

1057. A study in 2016 found that giant panda poo would make great fuel for an engine.

1063. Four-stroke engines, like those in cars, cannot run upside down, while two-stroke engines can.

1059. Most train locomotives are also hybrid electric vehicles.

1060. A hybrid electric vehicle like the Toyota Prius uses an internal combustion engine to generate electricity for an electric motor.

1061. The longer the power boat, the faster it is!

1062. The most expensive motorcycle is the Feline One – it costs $360,000!

1058. Some cars can be run on grease leftover from making french fries.

That's Bonkers!

ZOOM, ZOOM, ZOOM!

1064. A modern drag race car will use more fuel in one minute than most cars can carry in their tank. Good thing they only take a few seconds to get down the track!

1065. A gun is technically a type of internal combustion engine.

1066. It is very likely that kids in elementary school today will not be able to buy brand-new gasoline-powered cars as adults because there will be only electric cars available.

That's Bonkers!

108   *That's Bonkers!*

Chapter 27

GUTS AND GLORY

1067. The most popular sport on earth is soccer.

1070. Did you know that athletes did not wear clothes in the original Olympic games?

1072. In 1962 Wilt Chamberlain did what no one has been able to do since - score 100 points in a basketball game.

1068. Shaquille O'Neil, the famous basketball player, hit almost 12,000 baskets in his career; only 1 was a 3-pointer.

1071. The longest major league baseball game ever happened in 1984. Over two days, the White Socks and the Brewers played 25 innings, taking 8 hours and six minutes.

1073. One factory alone produces over 200 million ping pong balls every year.

1069. When basketball was invented, peach baskets were used as hoops, which is why they are called baskets.

1074. Snowboarding events were not in the winter Olympics until 1998.

That's Bonkers!

GUTS AND GLORY

1075. The first American footballs were made from the bladder of a pig or a sheep. That's why they call playing football "throwing the ol' pig skin."

1076. An astronaut hit a golf ball with a golf club on the moon, making golf the only sport played there.

1077. The United States has hosted more Olympic games than any other country.

1078. Baseball player Ray Caldwell was struck by lightning in the middle of a game in 1919 - and kept playing.

1079. A 1911 record set by baseball pitcher Cy Young has never been broken. He pitched 749 complete games in his career.

1080. Richard Petty won 200 NASCAR races in his career. That is almost double the second-place record holder, David Pearson, with 105 career wins.

1081. The rules of polo prohibit playing left-handed.

1082. The football team, Chicago Bears, once beat the Washington Redskins with a score of 73-0.

1083. A set of snow skis found in Norway are over 1,300 years old.

1084. Neither the people watching nor the people in the ring know who is winning a boxing match until after it is over.

1085. Over 220 million people in the world regularly play badminton.

1086. Brazil has won the most World Cup trophies in soccer, with 5. Italy and Germany are tied for second with 4.

1087. The Miami Dolphins football team played a completely undefeated season in 1972. They finally won the Super Bowl against the Dallas Cowboys.

1088. One professional tennis match lasted over 11 hours.

110

That's Bonkers!

GUTS AND GLORY

1089. Swimmer Michael Phelps has won 28 Olympic Gold Medals - more than any other Olympic athlete. Eight of those were in 2008, breaking the record of first-place finishes at one Olympic games.

1090. The first tennis rackets were made from sheep's intestines.

1091. The Olympic Games used to include a tug-of-war.

1092. Did you know that Mike Tyson became the youngest heavyweight boxing champion at just 20 years old?

1093. Once, the two tallest players in NBA history both played on the same team. They were 7 feet, 7 inches tall.

1094. Sprinter Usain Bolt holds the world record in both the 100 and 200-meter sprints, earning him the nickname Fastest Man on Earth.

1095. MLB pitcher Nolan Ryan threw 5,714 strikeouts in his career - 839 more than second-place pitcher Randy Johnson.

1096. Tiger Woods was the youngest person ever to win golf's Masters Tournament at 19 years old.

1097. In the 2017 Superbowl, the New England Patriots accomplished the greatest comeback in Super Bowl history. They were down 28-3 to the Atlanta Falcons at one point but still managed to pull out a win. Never give up!

1098. The 2001 Seattle Mariners won 116 of 162 baseball games but were still unable to make it to the World Series that year.

1099. Basketball player Wilt Chamberlain once scored 100 points in a single game.

That's Bonkers!

GUTS AND GLORY

1100. In bowling, it is called a 'turkey' if you get three consecutive strikes.

1101. Female golfer Michelle Wie became the youngest person to place in the top 10 of an LPGA tournament at age 13

1102. Did you know that the summer and winter Olympics never happen in the same year? But they both happen in even-numbered years.

That's Bonkers!

ARTSY FARTSY

Chapter 28

1108. Leonardo da Vinci wrote the most expensive book in the world. It sold for over $30 million.

1103. A flute made 60,000 years ago was found in a cave. It still plays music.

1109. Composer Wolfgang Amadeus Mozart wrote his first symphony when he was eight.

1104. Neanderthals made the oldest known painting 64,000 years ago.

1110. Procrastination is something most people struggle with, including Leonardo da Vinci! It took him 17 years to complete two of his most famous works.

1105. There are only 20 known paintings left by the artist Leonardo da Vinci.

1111. 1,700 of the words we use today were created by William Shakespeare.

1106. Would you believe that none of the band members of the Beatles knew how to read or write music?

1112. According to his mother, Pablo Picasso's first word was the Spanish word for 'pencil.'

1107. Every song except for one on Justin Timberlake's album 'Justified' was originally written for Michael Jackson.

That's Bonkers!

ARTSY FARTSY

1113. Artist Vincent Van Gogh once cut off his left ear. He later said he had no memory of the incident.

1114. Several video games are now displayed, in various formats, in the New York Museum of Modern Art.

1115. The rapper, Eminem, holds the world record for rapping 7.5 words per second. That's a whopping 1,560 words in 6 minutes!

1116. Salvador Dali's most famous painting features three watches that appear to be melting.

1117. Michelangelo hated painting the ceiling of the Sistine Chapel, and now it is one of his most famous works.

1118. Based on self-portraits, several famous artists had crossed eyes - a condition called strabismus. Da Vinci, Rembrandt, and Picasso all may have had the condition.

1119. World-famous artist Vincent van Gogh only sold one painting while he was alive.

1120. The current United States flag was designed by 17-year-old Robert G. Heft and was part of a school project. He only received a B- for his work.

1121. Unfortunately, many artists live lives of poverty and do not become famous until after their deaths.

1122. Everyone knows Eric Carle's book "The Very Hungry Caterpillar," right? Approximately one copy is sold per minute around the world!

1123. A Russian painting sold for $60 million at an auction in 2008. The painting consists of a single large red square on a white background.

1124. The author of the Captain Underpants books, Dav Pilkey, has dyslexia and ADHD. Captain Underpants is a story he created when he was in second grade.

1125. Hawaii has an official musical instrument, and it's the super cool ukulele!

114

That's Bonkers!

YOU ARE MY HERO

Chapter 29

1126. US Marine William Kyle Carpenter is the youngest person to be awarded the Medal of Honor. He threw himself on top of a live grenade to protect his fellow soldiers - and lived!

1127. Amelia Earhart was the first woman to fly across the Atlantic Ocean.

1128. A Boston Terrier nicknamed Sergeant Stubby became the most decorated war dog of the United States during World War I. Surprisingly, Stubby was smuggled into military life when a soldier hid him in his overcoat while shipping off to France!

1129. The word 'hero' comes from ancient Greece.

1130. A man in China became famous for standing in front of military tanks to stop them. No one knows who he was, but he has inspired millions.

1131. A 10-year-old boy, Kyle, saved his teacher from choking using the Heimlich manoeuvre that he had learned in Scouts.

1132. Polish fighter Witold Pilecki intentionally got himself arrested by the Nazis during World War II so that he could reveal what was going on there.

That's Bonkers!

YOU ARE MY HERO

1133. Dr. Jim O'Connell and a team of doctors voluntarily treat homeless patients living on the streets of Boston, Massachusetts.

1134. A pod of dolphins protected surfer Todd Endris from a shark attack. He probably would have died if it weren't for the dolphins.

1135. Rosa Parks helped the American civil rights movement with one simple act: she refused to give up her seat on a bus!

1136. A horse in the US Marines during the Korean War earned two Purple Hearts and one good conduct medal.

1137. Three lions guarded a 12-year-old girl in Ethiopia that was being kidnapped. They protected the girl until the police arrived.

1138. US actor Steve Buscemi rushed back to work as a New York fire-fighter in the days following the 9/11 attacks.

1139. Did you know that American actor, Vin Diesel, rescued a father and his two kids from a burning car after a car crash?

1140. During his service in World War II, US soldier Audie Leon Murphy won every medal of valor the US had. And some from a couple of other countries too.

1141. Mamoudou Gassama climbed outside a building four stories up to save a child hanging helplessly from a balcony.

1142. More than 300 search and rescue dogs helped find victims in the wreckage of the World Trade Center after the 9/11 attacks.

That's Bonkers!

YOU ARE MY HERO

1143. A woman choking on an apple was saved when her golden retriever Toby jumped on her chest, clearing the apple from her throat!

1144. Fire-fighters in Brooklyn, New York, watched as Scarlett the cat repeatedly rushed into a burning garage to rescue all of her kittens. She got severely burned, but her kittens survived because of her efforts.

1145. 11-year-old Orion Jean founded the Race for Kindness Foundation. The foundation donates meals, toys, and books to children in the United States.

1146. A high school basketball team saved a young girl that had been hit by a car and was trapped underneath it. The team had heard screams for help and ran to the scene and were able to lift the car enough to get her out.

1147. A pot-bellied pig named Lulu lay down in the road to stop traffic in order to get help for her owner. Her owner had a heart attack and needed immediate emergency help.

That's Bonkers!

118

That's Bonkers!

EXPLOSIONS AND ERUPTIONS
Chapter 30

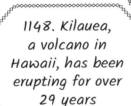

1148. Kilauea, a volcano in Hawaii, has been erupting for over 29 years

1150. All of Yellowstone Park is in the crater of a volcano. It is one of 12 known super-volcanoes on Earth.

1153. Scientists have seen eruptions on the moon of Jupiter.

1149. The largest recent volcanic explosion was Mount Tambora in Indonesia, 20 times larger than the eruption of Mt St Helens in Washington state, USA.

1151. Twenty different volcanoes erupt every single day.

1154. Australia is the only continent on Earth without a volcano.

1152. The large cracking sounds from a volcano eruption can travel hundreds of miles and do a lot of damage, like breaking glass and hearing loss.

1155. The United States detonated the very first hydrogen bomb, called Ivy Mike, in 1952.

That's Bonkers!

EXPLOSIONS AND ERUPTIONS

1156. There are over 100,000 lightning strikes on Earth every day, and thankfully, only around 15% cause a fire.

1157. The Chinese invented gunpowder.

1158. The most powerful artificial explosion in history was a 50-megaton nuclear bomb tested by Russia.

1159. Garbage dumps produce methane gas as the trash decomposes. This can lead to explosions if the gas isn't safely released.

1160. There are more than 1,500 volcanoes in the world considered active.

1161. A pilot in an emergency situation dropped an unexploded atomic bomb into the Caribbean Sea. The navy could not find it, and it is assumed to be buried in the mud under the sea.

1162. Over half of the volcanoes in the world are in a ring around the Pacific Ocean.

1163. The biggest non-nuclear explosion caused by man was a 4.2-kiloton explosion at the White Sands Missile Range in the United States.

1164. Did you know that the largest volcano in our solar system is on Mars?

1165. The Nobel Peace Prize was funded by the guy that invented dynamite.

1166. A sonic boom from a shock wave, not an explosion.

1167. In 2016, a fireworks explosion in Tultepec, Mexico, killed 42 people.

1168. A single solar flare releases more energy than all the nuclear bombs ever exploded.

120

That's Bonkers!

EXPLOSIONS AND ERUPTIONS

1169. There are two types of atomic bombs. A fission bomb splits atoms, and a fusion bomb squishes two atoms into one.

1170. The loudest sound heard by modern humans was when the Krakatoa volcano erupted in 1883.

1171. The Tunguska incident was the massive meteor explosion in the air above a remote Russian forest. The blast flattened over 80 million trees

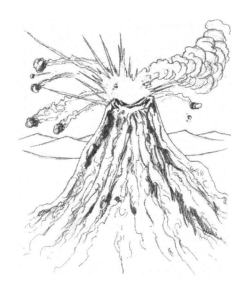

That's Bonkers!

That's Bonkers!

MASHED POTATOES

Chapter 31

1172. There are about 50,000 earthquakes every day.

1173. There is a sentence that uses every single letter in the English alphabet: "the quick brown fox jumps over the lazy dog."

1174. Did you know that a group of lemurs is called a "conspiracy?"

1175. The longest human beard ever recorded was over seventeen feet in length.

1176. Bamboo can grow 3 feet per day!

1177. There are almost 130 million books in the world.

1178. There is a way to never miss a high-five again. Simply look at the other person's elbow while high-fiving.

1179. A fire in a coal mine beneath Centralia, Pennsylvania, has been burning for over 40 years.

1180. Can you believe that the brain of an ostrich is smaller than one of its eyes?

That's Bonkers!

123

MASHED POTATOES

1181. The moon causes ocean tides.

1182. It is impossible to tickle yourself.

1183. There are more LEGO mini-figures on the planet than living people.

1184. The ridges on the sides of US coins are there to stop people from shaving thin bits of silver from the coins.

1185. There is only one state whose name is one-syllable - Maine.

1186. If you leave pearls in vinegar, they will melt.

1187. Rhubarb grows so fast that you can sometimes hear it make popping sounds.

1188. Most people cannot laugh on command, but it is contagious, and if you see someone laughing, it's usually pretty hard to resist the urge to laugh. Hahaha!

1189. Did you know there are more ways to shuffle a deck of cards than atoms in our solar system?

1190. Nearly 1 out of every four people in Europe died during The Black Plague.

1191. The index finger of the Statue of Liberty is eight feet long!

1192. Mount Everest may be the highest mountain in the world, but the tallest mountain is the island of Hawaii.

1193. Kangaroo rats rarely drink water. Most of their hydration is from the food they eat.

1194. It is legal to shoot and kill a BigFoot in Texas. (If you can find one!)

124

That's Bonkers!

MASHED POTATOES

1195. Believe it or not, an octopus has three hearts!

1196. There are more episodes of The Simpsons than any other television show made.

1197. Did you know that the little blob of toothpaste you squeeze onto your toothbrush is called a "nurdle"?

1198. There is a fear of being watched by ducks - Anatidaephobia!

1199. Mickey Mouse wasn't the first choice for a name. Originally he was to be named Mortimer. I'm glad they changed their mind!

1200. The King of Hearts in a deck of cards is called the suicide king because it looks like his sword is in his head.

1201. 80% of the living animals on earth are insects.

1202. Our solar system is over 4 1/2 billion years old.

1203. Did you know that 65% of people in the United States have Nomophobia? This is the fear of being without your smartphone.

1204. Over 1.5 million people work for McDonald's.

1205. Lightning and thunder always happen at the same time. The light just gets to us faster than the sound!

1206. The best-selling video game of all time - is Minecraft.

1207. Most of us laugh about 15 times a day.

1208. The plastic piece wrapped around a shoelace's end is called an aglet.

1209. The Monopoly game is the most played game worldwide and was originally invented by a woman.

That's Bonkers!

MASHED POTATOES

1210. Walt Disney did not allow his male employees to have mustaches.

1211. Body armor, like bullet-proof vests, can be made from spider web silk.

1212. Most people spend about 2 1/2 days every month looking for stuff they lost.

1213. Tiger roars were used for the movie "The Lion King" because lions' roars were not loud enough.

1214. 43% of all people born before 1800 died before the age of 5 years old.

1215. Some lucky people are unable to smell skunk spray.

1216. There is one animal that basically never dies. The Hydra is a sea creature that continually regenerates its cells.

1217. Saying OK probably comes from the phrase "All Correct" - intentionally misspelled to be funny.

1218. The United States used to have paper bills worth $100,000 each.

1219. The first thing bought in a supermarket by scanning its barcode was a pack of chewing gum. Clyde Dawson bought it in 1974.

1220. When it comes to the origin and history of April Fools' Day, historians don't really agree about how it started.

1221. The longest surgery ever recorded lasted 103 hours.

1222. Most people fall asleep in seven minutes.

1223. Spider silk is stronger than steel.

126

That's Bonkers!

MASHED POTATOES

1224. Trick or treat was likely first called out in 1927 in the province of Alberta, Canada.

1227. Can you believe that the average family of four loses around 60 socks per year?

1229. On average, four-year-old kids ask 400 questions per day!

1225. A pregnant goldfish is called a twit!

1228. It would take someone eight years, seven months, and six days of yelling to produce enough sound energy to heat one cup of Joe!

1230. Adults yawn approximately 20 times a day.

1226. A French prisoner invented mashed potatoes. He was trying to make the only food he got more interesting.

1231. In 1977, a 13-year-old found a tooth growing out of his left foot!

That's Bonkers!

128   That's Bonkers!

CONCLUSION

This is the end of our book, but do not be sad, as the world is a magical place filled with wonders and many more things for you to discover! We only scratched the surface here, and it is now up to you to keep your eyes and ears open to keep learning.

We hope you had as much fun reading the facts in this book as we had researching and writing them. We want to let you go with one of our favorite quotes:

"The beautiful thing about learning is that nobody can take it away from you."
- B.B. King

We all hope here at Smart Cookie Publishing that you learned a lot and that our book provided you with lots of fun and many hours of great reading.

We would be incredibly thankful if you could take just 60 seconds to write a brief review on Amazon.

Even if it's just a few words! That would mean the world to us and frankly, we might even do a little "happy dance" once we receive your review.

Customer Reviews

★★★★★ 15
5.0 out of 5 stars ▾

5 star		100%
4 star		0%
3 star		0%
2 star		0%
1 star		0%

Share your thoughts with othe

Write a customer review ◂

BYE!

That's Bonkers!

That's Bonkers!

Made in the USA
Las Vegas, NV
25 August 2023

76601548R00074